BRIAN TURNER'S FAVOURITE BRITISH RECIPES

Classic dishes from Yorkshire Pudding to Spotted Dick...

Classic and quirky chef Brian Turner is a household name throughout Britain, thanks to his regular television appearances. Here he brings you the best of British cooking in a collection of over 120 recipes. The recipes are spiced with fascinating insights into the history of some of our favourite dishes, and anecdotes of Brian Turner's experiences in cooking, from his dad's café to the Savoy!

BRIAN TURNER'S FAVOURITE BRITISH RECIPES

DEDICATION

To my mum and dad, sadly no longer with us, and to Louis Virot, my first mentor

Brian Turner's Favourite British Recipes

by

Brian Turner

Magna Large Print Books
Long Preston, North Yorkshire,
BD23 4ND, England.

British Library Cataloguing in Publication Data.

Turner, Brian
 Brian Turner's favourite British recipes.

A catalogue record of this book is
available from the British Library

ISBN   0-7505-2148-1

First published in Great Britain 2003
by Headline Book Publishing

Edited by Susan Fleming/Art direction by Lisa Pettibone/Home
economy by Annabel Ford/Styling by Roisin Nield/
Reprographics by Spectrum Colour, Ipswich

Published in Large Print 2004 by arrangement with
Headline Book Publishing Ltd.

Magna Large Print is an imprint of Library Magna Books Ltd.

Printed and bound in Great Britain by
T.J. (International) Ltd., Cornwall, PL28 8RW

Contents

Introduction

Although my basic training was in French cooking, and most years of my long career as well, I'm an Englishman born and proud of it. I grew up on classic British – Yorkshire – food. My mother cooked for us at home, mostly long-cooked stews and baked vegetables, and my father ran a transport café nearby. I used to help at the café, along with my brothers and sister, and could say that I was a head chef at the tender age of twelve! I'm still a dab hand at breakfasts, my speciality then. And my first professional job, at the age of eighteen, couldn't have been more British, as it was at that bastion of Englishness, Simpson's in the Strand. There I learned the vagaries of the catering trade, and eventually was allowed to carve the roasts in front of the customers, the ultimate accolade for a mere whipper-snapper from the kitchen.

So I am not unfamiliar with British food, and in fact when at home, I tend to cook things which are much more British in feel than French. But of course the history of cooking in this country has been as hybrid as the language: the Vikings influenced us, as did the French after 1066, and then later, when what seemed like all the French chefs decamped to London in the nineteenth century. It would appear that there have always been two strands of British cooking and eating: one for the rich in the cities who could absorb foreign influences (because they could afford it), and one for the poor in the north and west, who made do with what they could grow, pick, kill or poach (and the latter is not in the culinary sense). The differential between these strands is now far smaller than it was, because of modern communications and our burgeoning interest in food – although, sadly, some people will always eat less well than others. However different these traditions are, though, both are characteristically British, and both are reflected in this book, which will demonstrate, I hope, that you don't need to have money to eat well.

It's been a revelation researching the background of English, Scottish, Welsh and Irish cooking. I don't think I had quite appreciated how rich our agricultural heritage was, or how lucky we have always been to have such a wealth of indigenous produce. This ranges from the fish and seafood caught along our long coastlines, to the magnificent animals reared on the rich pastures, and the vegetables and fruit some native, lots introduced – grown in our fields.

Home cooking, in any country in the world, is always produce- and season-led. Although we may have lost sight of this slightly these days, because of the advent of the super-market culture, there is still an inherent knowledge and awareness of what is best when. Nothing could be more delicious than the first English asparagus or broad bean, or the first Scottish raspberry.

I have tried to celebrate the magnificence of what was and is British food in the recipes following. No-one has ever agreed as to the 'original' recipe for something in particular, and of course basics differ from country to country and from county to county, for British cooking is very regional indeed. (As are French and Italian cooking, but somehow we're much simpler here.) All of the recipes are easy (well, most), and all are based on what could be an original way of doing things, but often with a slightly modern or peculiarly Turner twist. I'm quite proud of them, and have thoroughly enjoyed the months of reading, inventing, testing and tasting.

Lastly, this is not a chef's book, although written by a chef, and may not always be appreciated by my fellow professionals. My work with Beefeater and Tesco has made me turn to ideas that are less 'cheffy' in nature and more domestic. And *Ready Steady Cook* has honed me in the fine art of cooking food

that people want to cook as well as eat –
something many chefs have lost sight of.
(Incidentally, why that programme is
criticised so much by the profession, I
cannot understand. Its premise is the same
as the chefs' most revered annual competition, 'Chef of the Year'.) And most chefs
wouldn't dare to admit, as I happily do, that
their favourite foods to eat at home are
basically very simple. I'm a great fan of
Welsh rarebit...

1

Soups

The words 'soups' and 'starters' signify 'first course of the meal' to us now, but the concept of 'courses' as we know them today is actually fairly recent. At one time dishes in a formal meal were served buffet style, all laid out on the table at the same time. (In fact, we've come full circle now, doing it again in Chinese restaurants, in tapas bars and at Greek mezze tables.) The intention was (and is) to visually impress – and at very grand meals, a groaning table would have been a spectacle indeed. However, there were many drawbacks to this *service à la française*. Diners would have to concentrate on the dishes in front of them only, or assert themselves and ask fellow guests or servants to pass them something they wanted from elsewhere (difficult if they were shy). And often, of course, the food would be cold by the time it was eaten, particularly soups. It was not until the nineteenth century that the Russian pattern of eating, *service à la russe*, was introduced and adopted. Foods were carved and plated at the sideboard, served to each diner in a set pattern, and our familiar 'course' system was born.

Soup became and still is a classic starter course, and indeed it can often serve as a complete meal in itself, as a lunch with bread, for instance. In the very earliest times in Britain, soup would have been just that, possibly the only meal the less well off would have all day. 'Pottage' was the early soup, a potful of water in which vegetables, pulses or grains and flavourings – and occasionally some meat, if you were lucky – would be boiled all together. Often the liquid and contents would be poured over bread to serve and this 'sop', as it was known, is probably the origin of the word 'soup' (from the French *'souper'*, to taste, as is 'pottage', an anglicisation of *'potage'*).

The soups here represent a variety of types. The Scotch broth is perhaps the nearest to the original pottage (and the Scottish porridge is a direct descendant of the medieval grain pottage). The others reveal how tastes gradually changed as new ingredients became available (the tomato and Jerusalem artichoke, for instance), and new influences were introduced (those of the immigrant French and, much later, those returning from India). Fish soup-stews are found all over Europe – think of the French bouillabaisse and garbure, for instance, and there are examples in Britain, from the north of Scotland to Wales to the south of Ireland.

Green Pea and Ham Soup

SERVES 8

The traditional English pea soup was made with dried peas, and its greeny-brown colour was so similar to the dense smog that dominated London in the winter (until as late as the 1960s), that the smog became known as a 'pea-souper'. In *Bleak House*, Dickens referred to the fog as the 'London Particular', and the name has been used for both fog and soup ever since.

There are so many versions of pea soup that to say one is the definitive classical recipe is practically impossible. Soup made from tinned peas is my least favourite but, if made from dried, fresh or a mixture, can work well. The following, however, is the one I like best. It will always remind me of the time Bob Holness came on *Ready Steady Cook*, and I made him some pea soup. This allowed the lovable Fern Britton to utter these immortal lines, 'can I have a "P" please, Bob?'

85g (3 oz) unsalted butter
1 large onion, peeled and finely diced
900g (2 lb) frozen peas
1 small bunch fresh mint, tied together
85g (3 oz) plain flour
300ml (10 fl oz) double cream
salt and freshly ground black pepper

Ham stock
1 ham hock, about 900g (2 lb) in weight
3.4 litres (6 pints) water
2 carrots, trimmed
2 onions, peeled
1 head celery, washed
12 black peppercorns
1 bay leaf

1 To start the stock, soak the hock for 12 hours in enough cold water to cover.

2 Drain off the soaking water, and cover the ham hock with the measured cold water. Bring to the boil and skim off any scum, then add the carrots, onions and celery, all whole. Leave to simmer gently for about 20 minutes, then add the peppercorns and bay leaf. Gently simmer for a further 1½-2 hours until the ham is cooked through. Watch it carefully: you don't want the liquid to reduce too much. Strain off the stock for the soup – you will need 1.7 litres (3 pints).

Put the ham to one side and discard the vegetables and flavourings.

3 Melt the butter in a heavy-bottomed pan, add the finely diced onion and half the frozen peas. Add the mint, and put the lid on the pan. Leave to gently stew for 3-5 minutes. At this point add the flour, and stir in carefully, possibly taking the pan off the heat to stop it sticking. Return the pan to the heat, and cook the pea roux for 2 minutes. Do not let it colour.

4 Slowly add the measured hot ham stock to the roux, beating well with a wooden spoon after each addition to get rid of any lumps of flour. When the stock is all added, make sure that the bottom of the pan is clear of everything. Leave to simmer for 20 minutes.

5 Meanwhile, blanch the remaining peas in boiling water for just 2 minutes. Plunge into a bowl of iced water, which will retain the bright green colour.

6 At the same time it is a good idea to take the skin from the ham hock, to take the meat from the bone and to carefully cut the latter into fine dice. Mix this ham with half of the blanched peas and keep to one side.

7 The soup is now cooked so take out the bunch of mint and put the remaining blanched peas (not those with the ham) into the soup. Liquidise the soup, and then I like to push it through a fine sieve or chinois (conical strainer).

8 When all is through, re-boil the soup gently, adding the double cream, and season as necessary. Put the reserved peas and ham into the soup, and serve immediately.

•It's not always easy to buy ham hocks these days, except from good butchers. You could use gammon instead (or bacon rinds tied up in muslin, for flavour). Use some boiled ham with peas in the soup at the end.

•A pea soup is not traditionally served with ham in it, but this addition makes for a much more gutsy dish.

•This soup is often served with toasted bread triangles, but I prefer it with croûtons, i.e. fried bread dice.

•Pea soup is great chilled with perhaps extra cream and chopped mint. The French serve stewed lettuce and baby onions with their pea soup.

Cock-a-Leekie

SERVES 4–6

Cock-a-leekie is as much associated in people's minds with Scotland as haggis is, and why the Scots should use prunes always puzzled me. But in fact the soup made from chicken, leeks and prunes is a variant on a dish that occurs elsewhere in Britain, in Wales and Lancashire particularly. The dish from Lancashire is known as Hindle Wakes, probably deriving from 'Hen de la Wake', referring to the holiday Wakes Week in the cotton areas of the country; this is a boiled chicken stuffed with prunes and coated with a bright yellow lemon sauce. It was thought to have been introduced by weavers coming in from Belgium in the fourteenth century, and the dried fruit is a familiar addition to many medieval dishes throughout Europe.

Whatever its history, it is a good family soup-meal, similar to a pot-au-feu. You can use a tough old boiling fowl if you like, probably traditional, and once a capon would have been ideal. Beef stock was usually used to cook the chicken in; I've added the beef to give just a further Scottish taste dimension.

450g (1 lb) topside of beef
1.2 litres (2 pints) chicken stock
900g (2 lb) leeks
1 sprig each fresh parsley and thyme
1 small chicken, approx. 900g (2 lb) in
  weight
12 large prunes, soaked if necessary
salt and freshly ground black pepper

1 Put the beef into a large pot and add the chicken stock. Bring to the boil and allow to simmer for 20 minutes. Skim off any scum that comes to the top.

2 Meanwhile, trim and wash the leeks, discarding the coarsest of the dark green leaves. Slice the leeks finely.

3 Add the parsley and thyme to the pot along with half of the sliced leeks, and leave to simmer for an hour.

4 Take the meat out and put into a clean pot. Strain the stock over the meat to remove the leeks and herbs. Put the chicken into the pot and make sure it is covered with stock; if not, top up with water. Simmer until the chicken is nearly cooked, about 40 minutes. Test by piercing one of its thighs with a roasting fork: the juices should run slightly pink.

5 Add the prunes and the rest of the leeks, and simmer for a further 20 minutes. Check for seasoning.

6 Take the beef and chicken out of the liquid. Take the chicken meat from the bone, and remove and discard the skin. Chop the meat into large chunks. Slice the beef thinly.

7 Divide the beef, chicken, leeks, prunes and hot stock between warmed bowls, and serve immediately.

•Once, making something like this would have been the way of life, putting a slow-cooking stew or soup on in the morning, and getting on with everything else – feeding the chickens, hoeing the vegetables. washing the clothes – in the meanwhile. You could still do that today, if you just have the right attitude – think about it in advance, and with a few glances at the pot every now and again, you can get on with the ironing, or read a book or watch television. In fact it's really therapeutic...

•Prunes can come pre-soaked, in which case all you need to do is add them to the soup (they will be identified as such on the packet). But traditionally dried prunes will need soaking in plenty of water to cover at least for a couple of hours, and preferably overnight.

Cullen Skink

SERVES 4

'Cullen skink' means a soup-stew which comes from Cullen, a village on the coast of the Moray Firth in Scotland. It is typical coastal fare – dishes like this are traditional throughout Europe – but the difference lies in the smoked fish used. Scotland was the centre of fish smoking, and the fish once used would have been an Arbroath smokie or a Finnan haddock (from the Aberdeenshire village of Findon).

Nick Nairn, Paul Rankin and myself were being taught to drive off-road in the latest brand-new Range Rover, in a programme for the BBC. Our pay-back was that in front of the cameras we would cook a Scottish-type menu, devised by the aforesaid Mr Nairn. He took us through the method for Cullen Skink, and this is a slightly sophisticated variant of his, and the original, using hard-boiled egg and potato to thicken and to add flavour, colour and goodness.

675g (1½ lb) natural, rather than dyed, smoked haddock
25g (1 oz) unsalted butter
300ml (10 fl oz) fish stock or water
salt and freshly ground white pepper
2 hard-boiled eggs, shelled
115g (4 oz) cooked mashed potato
850ml (1½ pints) milk
300ml (10 fl oz) single cream
1 tbsp chopped fresh chives or parsley

1 Preheat the oven to 180°C/350°F/Gas 4.

2 Make sure all the pin bones are taken out of the fish. Use pliers or tweezers.

3 Butter a suitable ovenproof dish, and lay the cut smoked haddock in it, along with the stock or water. Season, put into the pre-heated oven, and bake for 10 minutes.

4 Take out of the oven and drain, keeping the liquid. Take the flesh off the skin. Discard the skin.

5 Put half the fish in a bowl with the shelled hard-boiled eggs and the mashed potato. Purée this together using a wooden spoon or a pestle. Mix the milk into this, then the cream and strained fish-cooking stock, stirring all well together

6 Pour into a pan and bring to the boil. If necessary, strain.

7 Add the rest of the flaked fish and the chives or parsley to the soup, check the seasoning and serve hot.

Oxtail Soup

SERVES 4

People categorise oxtail as offal, but it is actually an appendage rather than an internal organ, and has a concentrated meaty flavour and texture no organ meat has. We think of oxtail soup and stew as being quintessentially English, but some claim that the inspiration was French: Huguenots fleeing persecution in the seventeenth century settled in East London and had to make their daubes and stews from the cheapest meat available (the tails of the cattle used by the East End tanners). The fame of the soup spread thereafter throughout the country.

675g (1½ lb) meaty oxtail
salt and freshly ground black pepper

25g (1 oz) plain flour
55g (2 oz) beef dripping (or lard)
2 medium onions, peeled and finely
 chopped
1 large carrot, peeled and finely chopped
4 celery stalks, finely chopped
1 tbsp tomato paste
1.7 litres (3 pints) water or stock
25g (1 oz) unsalted butter
1 tbsp chopped fresh parsley

1 Get the butcher to cut the oxtail between the bones and through the cartilage. Dry off the meat, then season and coat lightly in flour.

2 Heat the dripping until quite hot in a large saucepan, then colour all sides of the oxtail in the fat. Add half the onion and all of the carrot and celery to the oxtail, and colour lightly. Stir in the tomato paste and fry gently for a few minutes. Add the water or stock and bring up to the boil. Cover and simmer for up to 3 hours when the meat is ready to drop off the bones.

3 Take the oxtail out and pick off the meat. Trim off the fat, then throw the bones and fat away, keeping the meat separate. Strain off the liquor and put into the fridge overnight. The next day remove the fat that has set on top and throw this away as well.

(This may all seem time-consuming and over-laborious, but I assure you it's well worth it.)

4 Melt the butter in a clean saucepan, add the remaining chopped onion, and sweat until softened. Add the diced oxtail meat and then the strained, defatted stock. Bring to the boil, and reduce to taste. Check the seasoning, and serve sprinkled with the chopped parsley.

Jerusalem Artichoke Soup

SERVES 4

What I love about this soup is its silky smooth texture and subtle flavour. It is also known as Palestine soup, presumably because of the vegetable used, Jerusalem artichokes. These were introduced to Europe by French explorers of Canada in the sixteenth century, and were known first as the 'potatoes of Canada'. The name 'Jerusalem' actually comes from a corruption of the Italian word *'girasole'*, sunflower, as the vegetable plant is a member of the same family (*Helianthus*). The 'artichoke' bit is just as odd: the Jerusalem artichoke is a tuber, but it does have leaf and stalk growth of up to 3 metres high, as does the globe artichoke. Some say, too, that the flavour of the two artichokes is similar, but I cannot see it.

Try and buy large Jerusalem artichokes, as they will be easier to peel (they are very knobbly). If you don't want to be too sophisticated, just wash the tubers and cook them unpeeled, then sieve; the colour will be different, but the flavour will be just as good.

450g (1 lb) Jerusalem artichokes
salt and freshly ground black pepper
juice of 1 lemon
1 small onion, peeled and finely chopped
1 garlic clove, peeled and crushed
55g (2 oz) celery, chopped
55g (2 oz) unsalted butter
115g (4 oz) smoked bacon rinds, or 2 thick rashers smoked bacon
1.2 litres (2 pints) chicken or vegetable stock
300ml (10 fl oz) double cream
2 egg yolks

1 Choose artichokes that are not too knobbly wherever possible. Peel them: I like to use a small knife or potato peeler. Slice finely and, if not using straightaway, keep in cold water with some salt and the lemon juice to stop them from discolouring. Mix

27

the drained sliced artichokes with the onion, garlic and celery.

2 Melt the butter in a saucepan, and add the vegetables and bacon rinds (perhaps tied together with string for ease of removal) or bacon. Sweat carefully over a low heat with a lid on the pan, not allowing anything to colour

3 Add the stock, bring up to the boil, and simmer until the vegetables are cooked, about 15-20 minutes.

4 Take out the bacon rinds or bacon. Put the mixture through a liquidiser and then pass through a fine chinois or sieve, which makes for a creamy, velvety soup. Put back into a clean pan and add half the double cream. Bring to the boil, and season with salt and pepper.

5 Mix the egg yolks and the remaining double cream in a bowl. Pour some of the hot soup on to this mixture, stirring all the time. Put back into the pan and heat gently, but do not boil. Check the seasoning, and serve immediately.

•Croûtons and parsley are good garnishes. Another thing I like to do is roast or grill some almonds and then add two-thirds of them along with the vegetables (at stage 2). This adds flavour, then you sprinkle the remainder over the top of the soup when serving to add texture.

•If you've ever wondered what to do with the rinds you cut off bacon, well, use them for flavour as here. Freeze them each time you cut them off your breakfast rasher, and you will soon have enough to use.

•In stage 5 I tell you to pour some of the hot soup into the cold cream. Always do it this way round, hot into cold. If cold went into hot, the cold would curdle (i.e. the proteins would set), whereas the hot going into the cold just makes the cold a little warmer...

•To bring this soup bang up to date, you could froth it up at the last minute with one of those new-fangled hand blenders to make a cappuccino-style first course. We did this in 1975 at the Capital Hotel, so eat your heart out, Gordon Ramsay!

Mulligatawny Soup

SERVES 4

I first encountered this soup when I worked at Simpson's in the Strand (my first job, at the tender age of eighteen). It was popular, along with the infamous Brown Windsor soup, with gentlemen of a certain age who had presumably served in India at some time, and learned to love the heat and pepperiness of the cuisine. For the soup and its name are both relics of the Raj, the word 'mulligatawny' coming from two Tamil words meaning 'pepper' and 'water', the nearest thing to soup in India. It was originally a vegetarian sauce apparently, but the British adapted it to include all manner of flavourings and garnishes: the basic pepper water could be served with side bowls of cooked rice, lime wedges, grated coconut, crispy bacon pieces, sliced chillies and hard-boiled eggs.

This version here is a little posher, but lacks the extras!

55g (2 oz) unsalted butter
2 chicken thighs

1 apple, peeled, cored and finely diced
2 small onions, peeled and finely chopped
4 tomatoes, seeded and diced
1 tbsp Madras curry powder
1.2 litres (2 pints) lamb stock
1 tbsp mango chutney, chopped
4 tbsp cooked basmati rice
salt and freshly ground black pepper

1 Melt the butter in a saucepan, add the chicken thighs, allow them to colour lightly, then turn down the heat.

2 Add the diced apple and chopped onion to the pan, then the tomato dice. Do not allow the vegetables to colour. Sprinkle the curry powder over and fry carefully to release its flavour. Do not let it burn.

3 Now add the stock and bring up to the boil, lower the heat and simmer for about 40 minutes.

4 Take the chicken out of the soup, and remove and discard the bones and skin. Cut the meat into dice and put back into the soup along with the chopped mango chutney. Add the rice, warm through briefly, and check for seasoning. Serve hot.

•The soup in Simpsons was passed through a sieve, even the mango chutney, so that all you got in the pepper water was chicken and rice.

•You could make the soup with coconut milk instead of stock or half and half and grind your own spices such as cumin and coriander for curry powder, but you must have some heat – preferably chilli powder or a fresh chilli or two.

•Some versions of the recipe use scrag end of lamb instead of the chicken.

•Its often easier to put the rice straight into the cups or bowls, then pour the soup on top.

Scotch Broth

SERVES 4

Also known as barley broth, this soup is simple, but very satisfying, its only necessities being some lamb, barley and vegetables. Barley has become very fashionable nowadays, and many rated restaurants serve barley risottos or pilaffs, but it was a staple in Scotland from very early times, as indeed it was throughout much of the northern hemisphere. It has a good flavour and texture, and here it thickens the broth.

Apparently the famous and acerbic English writer, Dr Johnson, was not too fond of Scotland despite the Gaelic origins of his companion, James Boswell, but did actually approve of Scotch broth!

675g (1½ lb) scrag end or shoulder of
  lamb, cut into large pieces
55g (2 oz) good pearl barley
1.7 litres (3 pints) cold water
1 bouquet garni (parsley, thyme, bay leaf,
  black peppercorns)
1 medium onion, peeled and finely diced
2 leeks, cleaned and finely diced
2 carrots, trimmed and finely diced
4 celery stalks, finely diced
1 small white turnip, scrubbed and finely
  diced
85g (3 oz) shredded cabbage
salt and freshly ground black pepper
1 tbsp chopped fresh parsley

1 Trim the lamb of excess fat.

2 Put the barley into a large saucepan and add the water, then the lamb. Bring up to the boil and put in the bouquet garni. Cover with a lid, but use a wooden spoon to make sure the lid doesn't close properly, and simmer for about 1½ hours, taking off the scum regularly. (If you don't use a spoon,

it'll boil over and make an awful mess on the top of your stove.) Stir occasionally as well to make sure the barley doesn't stick.

3 Add the onion, leek, carrot, celery and turnip to the pan, and simmer for about 10 minutes. Take out the meat and dice it.

4 Put the meat back into the pan with the shredded cabbage. Cook for 5-10 minutes more. Check the seasoning, add the parsley and serve.

Cream of Mushroom Soup

SERVES 4

Mushroom soups appear in most cuisines, and on the continent they would probably be made with wild mushrooms. Here in Britain, however, we seem to have always been a little timid about most fungi, apart from cultivated ones. We took to cultivating them quite early, though, in the mid-eighteenth century, following the example of the French. Around Paris, mushrooms were cultivated in disused quarries; in England, stone mines near Bath were utilised. (In fact, the slightly larger button mushrooms on sale today are still called Paris mushrooms in the trade.)

Field mushrooms have the most intense flavour for a soup, but because of the dark gills, the colour is not good. Use button mushrooms instead, and serve with croûtons if you like.

55g (2 oz) unsalted butter
1 medium onion, peeled and finely
  chopped
1 medium leek, cleaned and finely
  chopped
450g (1 lb) button mushrooms, wiped and
  finely sliced
1 bouquet garni (thyme, parsley, in a leek
  leaf)
850ml (1 ½pints) chicken or vegetable
  stock, or both
salt and freshly ground black pepper
300ml (10 fl oz) double cream

Garnish
25g (1 oz) unsalted butter
115g (4 oz) button mushrooms, finely
  diced
1 tbsp chopped fresh parsley

1 Melt the butter in a large pan, and sweat the onion and leek – do not colour – for 5 minutes. Add the mushrooms to the pan, and sweat for another 5 minutes, but still do not colour

2 Add the bouquet garni, stock and some seasoning, bring to the boil and simmer for 30 minutes. Remove any scum that appears during the cooking.

3 Meanwhile, for the garnish, melt the butter, add the mushrooms and sauté gently. Do not colour them. Season, add the parsley and put to one side.

4 Remove the bouquet garni and liquidise the soup. Put into a clean pan, bring back to the boil, then add the double cream and seasoning to taste.

5 Add the mushroom and parsley mixture, and serve.

Chunky Tomato Soup

SERVES 4

Soup is one of the most traditional of dishes on the British culinary scene, and local 'pot' vegetables were used in the beginning, perhaps with a little grain or, when they were lucky, some meat. When tomatoes gradually came to be accepted, some two centuries or so after they had been introduced from the New World, they were pounded to make soups or acid sauces or ketchups (see page 307). Apparently it wasn't until the twentieth century that we were brave enough to eat these scarlet imports raw!

55g (2 oz) unsalted butter
115g (4 oz) each of carrots, peeled onion
  and celery, finely chopped
2 garlic cloves, peeled and finely chopped
675g (1½ lb) tomatoes, roughly chopped
basil stalks (**see below**)
a handful of parsley stalks
1 tbsp chopped fresh thyme
a pinch of unrefined caster sugar
salt and freshly ground black pepper
1.2 litres (2 pints) chicken stock
150ml (5 fl oz) single cream

Garnish
10 tomatoes, skinned and seeded (use
  skins and seeds in the soup, so do this
  first)
a splash of olive oil
a bunch of fresh basil, chopped (use the
  stalks in the soup)
1 garlic clove, peeled and chopped

1 Melt the butter in a large pan, and sweat the finely chopped carrot, onion and celery together. Do not colour. After 3 minutes, add the garlic, the skins and seeds of the garnish tomatoes, and the chopped tomatoes, along with the basil stalks, parsley stalks, thyme, sugar and some salt and pepper to taste. Stew gently for about 10 minutes.

2 When almost all of the liquid has disappeared, add the chicken stock, and cook gently for a further 20 minutes. Pass the soup and vegetables through a sieve.

3 Put back into a clean pan and bring back to the boil. Add the cream and check the seasoning.

4 Chop the skinned garnish tomatoes into neat dice. Warm them in the splash of oil with the basil and garlic. Pour into the soup and serve, with a swirl of cream if desired.

Chicken Noodle Soup

SERVES 8

We are famous in this country for making broths or stocks. They were the basis of early pottages, and still add savour to soups and sauces today. The French went one step further, clarifying broths to make consommé, and our clear British soups are probably a borrowing from across the channel. Almost anything can be used to make a consommé – meat, fish, mushrooms or tomatoes – but the most common is chicken. The classic British clear soup is chicken noodle soup, and the addition of the noodles is probably yet another borrowing, from the Jewish tradition – the *lokshen* (vermicelli) added to the chicken soup known colloquially as 'Jewish penicillin'.

450g (1 lb) raw chicken leg meat, off the bone
115g (4 oz) each of prepared carrot, leek, onion and celery, chopped
4 tomatoes, chopped
4 egg whites
salt
10 black peppercorns
2.4 litres (4 pints) good chicken stock
85g (3 oz) thin noodles or vermicelli
1 tbsp chopped fresh parsley
2 cold poached chicken breasts, skinned and finely diced

1 Chop the chicken leg meat up roughly, and mix with the chopped vegetables. Put all through a coarse mincer. Add the tomatoes.

2 Put this mixture into a heavy-bottomed

pan, then mix in the egg whites, some salt and the peppercorns. Add 300ml (10 fl oz) of the cold stock, and mix together. Add the rest of the stock and mix well with a large wooden spoon.

3 Put on to a gentle heat and slowly bring up to the boil, stirring regularly. The proteins in the egg white and chicken will set like a 'cake' on the bottom of the pan. As this cake cooks, it will start to rise in one piece, lifting all the sediment in the stock with it to the top. It's at this moment that care must be taken. As the liquid starts to boil, move the pan to the side, half on and half off the heat, and lower the heat. Try to ensure that the crust is broken on one side only, with the liquid gently simmering through this break. You want to keep it ticking over.

4 At this stage, leave the stock to cook for about 2 hours, uncovered, Taste will tell you when this is ready. It should be lipsmackingly savoury.

5 Carefully strain the majority of the liquid through a folded piece of muslin. Strain the last bit separately, as it might contain some debris which could spoil the bulk of the stock. Degrease the resultant stock using kitchen paper.

6 When you want to serve the soup, season the clarified stock and bring it back to a gentle boil. At the same time, cook the noodles or vermicelli in separate boiling salted water until just cooked. Strain and rinse under cold gently running water.

7 Add the noodles or vermicelli to the stock, along with the parsley and diced chicken. Warm through briefly, then serve.

•The first secret of a good consommé is the strength of the original stock. If you've got a good strong food processor or mincer, you could put the chicken legs, bones and all, through it, and use that as the clarifying agent, along with the egg whites, for a much more intense flavour. (This works well with fish too but not obviously, with the red meats.)

•Some people like long noodles, some like short, but it's really down to you. As its a soup, short pieces are probably better – simply break the noodles or vermicelli in your hands before cooking them. I do so in separate boiling water to get rid of the starch which might spoil the clarity of the consommé.

2

Eggs, Cheese and Savouries

'White meats' – the collective name for milk, milk products such as cheese, and egg – were the food of the poor in medieval times. Unable to afford much red meat, the products of the precious family cow and chickens would have provided important protein in the diet. The eggs would have been cooked very simply: 'roasted', 'poached' and served with collops of bacon (the early form of today's bacon and eggs), or mixed into a grain porridge. The rich would have used eggs in much more sophisticated ways – in pies, custards, and puddings both savoury and sweet. Later people ate buttered or scrambled eggs, or boiled them in their shells. It surprised me to learn how long it was before the 'foaming' and 'raising' qualities of egg whites were recognised – not until about the late seventeenth century. Thereafter, eggs were used much more widely, particularly in sweet puddings and cakes (see Chapters Seven and Eight).

When I was young, after the war, we had a

few chickens in the back garden (as did many a family then), and I used to hate going to collect the eggs, as the hens would peck me! However, I enjoyed eating what I collected (and the chickens themselves occasionally).

Centuries ago the cheese eaten by the poor would have been hard, and local, for not until transport and communications improved did different varieties of cheese become familiar elsewhere in the country. Today, of course, cheese is available in all forms and from all over the world. There's actually been a revolution in Britain: once we only had nine hard cheeses, but now small producers are bringing out some wonderful varieties – fresh, soft and hard – available locally or from farmers' markets. It seems so bizarre, when one of our greatest leaders, Winston Churchill, criticised the French by saying we could never trust a nation that would produce a cheese for every day of the year...

Mrs Beeton wrote that cheese 'is only fit for sedentary people, as an after-dinner stimulant, and in very small quantity'. Which is why the category 'savouries' is here, as many are made with cheese. The savoury is, like afternoon tea, uniquely British and seems to have appeared at some time in the nineteenth century.

Baked Eggs

SERVES 4

I've given you two versions of baked eggs here. The first is the equivalent of *'oeufs sur le plat'* , but I'm sure we have been preparing eggs like this for far longer than the French... (It's also known as 'shirred' eggs, which suggests 'scrambling' to me.) The second is slightly posher, more like an egg pudding or unrisen soufflé.

Version One

55g (2 oz) unsalted butter
8 eggs
salt and freshly ground black pepper

1 Preheat the oven to 200°C/400°F/Gas 6.

2 Melt a quarter of the butter in each of four flat, eared heatproof dishes of 6cm (2½ in) in diameter. Do not let it colour. Season the dish.

3 Break two eggs per person, one each into separate cups, then carefully pour into the

seasoned dishes.

4 Heat on the top of the stove, turning the dishes round to get an even heat, and then put into the preheated oven to set to the desired degree, about 3-4 minutes.

Version Two

55g (2 oz) unsalted butter
8 fresh eggs
150ml (5 fl oz) single cream
2 tbsp chopped fresh parsley
salt and freshly ground black pepper

1 Preheat the oven to 200°C/400°F/Gas 6.

2 Melt the butter and put into an oven-proof pie dish, swirling well to coat all sides.

3 Beat the eggs, cream and parsley together, and season with salt and pepper.

4 Pour the eggs into the pie dish and put into a bain-marie of warm water. Bake in the preheated oven until set, about 8-10 minutes. Spoon out and serve.

•Both make good snacks, and of course

you could tart them up as a starter, lining the dishes with cooked mushrooms, tomatoes, spinach or smoked haddock. I first encountered the idea when I worked in Switzerland; baked eggs were served for breakfast, but on top of slices of cooked ham. (In the kitchen, we cooked this for ourselves in a huge frying pan: sliced sausage then sliced ham with twelve eggs broken on top. We'd eat from the pan.)

•Use bacon fat instead of butter in both recipes for extra flavour.

Cheesed Eggs

SERVES 4

This is very reminiscent of school days to me, when the only thing they could do properly was a cheese sauce (and no-one can go too far wrong with hard-boiled eggs). Something as simple as this would once have tasted particularly good because of the quality of the eggs, but you can come near if you use the best fresh, free-range and organic eggs you can find. A good Montgomery Cheddar cheese would be delicious.

8 fresh eggs
150ml (5 fl oz) cheese sauce, made with
  single cream (see page 212)
25g (1 oz) unsalted butter
salt and freshly ground black pepper
115g (4 oz) Cheddar, grated
2 egg yolks

1 Boil the eggs for 10 minutes then rest them for 30 minutes in cold water, shell and then slice (a machine for this is perfect).

2 Meanwhile, preheat the oven to 200°C/400°F/Gas 6, and make the cheese sauce.

3 Butter an ovenproof dish well and then season it. Arrange the eggs carefully in the bottom of the dish and season again. Sprinkle with 25g (1 oz) of the grated cheese.

4 Beat the egg yolks into the warm cheese sauce, and pour over the eggs. Sprinkle with the rest of the cheese. Season with pepper and bake in the preheated oven for 10 minutes. Brown the cheesy top under a preheated grill, then serve with lots of bread.

•The French have a similar dish to this, called *oeufs à la chimay*. The cooked yolks are pounded with mushroom duxelles, and stuffed into the white, then coated with the cheese (sorry, Mornay) sauce.

•This very grown-up dish is on the children's menu at the Brian Turner Restaurant at the Crowne Plaza NEC Hotel in Birmingham.

Scotch Eggs

MAKES 6

These sausagemeat-wrapped eggs, served for breakfast or as a snack in Scotland, stood alone, I thought, with no obviously similar dishes existing in other cuisines. Some sources have suggested, however, that there is an association with the Indian Moghul 'kofta', which consists of pounded spiced meat wrapped round savoury fillings, sometimes eggs. How the idea came to Scotland, no-one seems to know, but it could be something to do with men returning from service in India during the days of the Raj.

6 hard-boiled eggs (8-10 minutes)
55g (2 oz) plain flour

salt and freshly ground black pepper
350g (12 oz) sausagemeat
115g (4 oz) boiled ham, very finely
  chopped
2 eggs, beaten
115g (4 oz) fresh white breadcrumbs
vegetable oil for deep-frying

1 Shell the eggs and dry in a clean cloth. Season the flour with salt and pepper. Dip the eggs in this and shake off the excess.

2 Mix the sausagemeat and ham together, and split this mixture into six even parts. Flatten out in your hands to make a meat coating for each egg. Cover each egg with a portion of this mixture, pressing well at the joins to seal.

3 Dip the coated eggs into the seasoned flour again, and shake off the excess. Dip into the beaten egg and finally into the breadcrumbs to coat completely.

4 Re-shape at this stage, and put into the fridge for 10 minutes.

5 Deep-fry in moderately hot fat for about 10 minutes, turning as they cook. Take out, drain well and serve hot or cold.

•Try making the recipe with hard-boiled

quails' eggs. Very fiddly, but great for a canapé.

•Many recipes use only sausagemeat, but the addition of ham as well is occasionally found. Try Parma ham, an interesting substitute for boiled ham. And of course you could spice things up by adding some chopped fresh herbs or spices, such as chilli or cayenne, to the mixture.

Omelette Arnold Bennett

SERVES 1

Arnold Bennett based his 1930 novel, *Imperial Palace*, on the Savoy Hotel, where he often ate, and his fictional chef, Roho, on Jean-Baptiste Virlogeux, the then *chef de cuisine*. In return, Virlogeux invented this classic marriage of smoked haddock, eggs and cheese.

We made it during my time at the Capital Hotel, and when Egon Ronay once accused us of not changing the menu often enough, I quoted a sad but true story. A Norwegian customer had had this omelette twice on the trot, he liked it so much, and when he went home, he asked his wife to recreate the dish for him. The result was so unlike our original that he brought her straight back on a plane to London. However, we'd changed the menu that very day, so to satisfy his – and her – needs we had to change it back again and make the dish for him!

3 eggs
salt and freshly ground black pepper
15g (½ oz) unsalted butter
85g (3 oz) cooked smoked haddock
3 tbsp double cream
40g (1½ oz) Gruyère cheese, grated

1 Break the eggs into a bowl and beat, then season.

2 Melt the butter in your omelette pan, then add the eggs. Stir regularly until the eggs set. Keep lifting the sides up to make sure the eggs don't stick.

3 When the eggs are cooked enough, but still a little wet, add the smoked haddock. Put the pan under the preheated grill to set the rest of the eggs.

4 In the meantime make the creamy cheese sauce. Reduce the double cream until it begins to thicken, and take off the heat. Season and stir in 25g (1 oz) of the cheese.

5 Turn the omelette over on to a plate. Using the back of a spoon, spread the sauce over the top. Sprinkle with the remaining cheese and put under the preheated grill to brown. Serve immediately.

All-day Breakfast Bap

SERVES 8

The English breakfast is famous the world over, with its egg, bacon, sausage, fried tomato, fried mushroom and fried bread – cholesterol on a plate! Done well, though, it is delicious, but I have played around with the basic idea here to come up with something completely different.

The egg, bacon, sausage, tomato and mushroom are served together in a bun, rather like a burger, with lots of different seasonings to taste. I've even added some cheese. It tastes wonderful, at any time of the day!

8 bread buns

Filling
450g (1 lb) Cumberland or Lincolnshire
  sausages

salt and freshly ground black pepper
6 slices best-quality back bacon
vegetable oil
8 button mushrooms
25g (1 oz) butter
3 hard-boiled eggs, shelled and roughly
  chopped
5 sun-blush tomatoes, cut into fine strips
a handful of fresh parsley, finely chopped
1 tbsp tomato ketchup, bought or home
  made (see page 305)
1 tbsp brown sauce
55g (2 oz) Cheddar, grated (optional)

1 Remove the outer skin from the sausages, and put the meat in a bowl. Season with salt and pepper, gently mix together, and place to one side.

2 Discard the rinds, and cut the bacon rashers into lardons. Fry in a hot pan in 1 tbsp of the oil until golden brown. Drain and cool.

3 Remove the stalks from the mushrooms and cut them and the caps into quarters. Gently fry in the butter and another tbsp of oil. Season and cook until just done. Cool.

4 Incorporate all the ingredients into the sausagemeat and mix well together.

5 Shape the mixture into eight equal-sized patties and store in the fridge for half an hour or so before cooking.

6 To cook, heat a couple of tbsp of oil in a frying pan, to a moderate-high temperature. Add the patties, in batches if necessary; and seal both sides. Cook through well, for about 4-6 minutes each side.

7 Meanwhile, warm the buns through in a low oven, and butter them if you like (I don't). Serve a hot breakfast patty in each bun.

Cheese Pudding

SERVES 4

Very few people make things like this now, but once they would have been a major part of the diet – the protein of the cheese and eggs bulked out with bread. The first version here is a classic Welsh dish, but similar puddings were once known to be popular in East Anglia. If the first is like a savoury bread and butter pudding (something my father used to love – he would have had onions with it), the second is like a savoury queen of puddings.

Version One

6 slices stale bread
55g (2 oz) unsalted butter
salt and freshly ground black pepper
225g (8 oz) mature Cheddar, grated
1 tsp French mustard
freshly grated nutmeg and cayenne pepper
300ml (10fl oz) milk
300ml (10fl oz) single cream
2 eggs

1 Preheat the oven to 180°C/350°F/Gas 4.

2 Toast the bread on one side only. Use a little of the butter to grease an ovenproof pie dish, then season it. Take the crusts off the bread, and butter the untoasted side of the bread. Cut each slice into three rectangular pieces each.

3 Place a layer of buttered toast, toasted side down, into the greased pie dish. Mix the cheese with the mustard and some salt, nutmeg and cayenne, and sprinkle over the bread. Lay on more toast, buttered side up, and sprinkle with more cheese. Continue until everything has been used up, finishing with a layer of cheese.

4 Warm the milk and cream together. Beat the eggs to a froth, then strain into the milk. Mix well and pour over the bread.

5 Bake in the preheated oven for 30-40 minutes. Serve hot.

Version Two

115g (4 oz) unsalted butter
salt and freshly ground black pepper
300 ml (10 fl oz) single cream
150 ml (5 fl oz) milk
115g (4 oz) fresh breadcrumbs
1 tsp English mustard
225g (8 oz) mature Cheddar, grated
3 eggs

1 Use some of the butter to grease a pie dish of about 850ml (1½ pint) capacity. Season with black pepper.

2 Bring the cream and milk to the boil, then add 55g (2 oz) of the butter. Season the breadcrumbs and mix with the mustard in a bowl, then pour in the hot cream mixture. Cover and leave to stand for 20 minutes.

3 Meanwhile, preheat the oven to 200°C/400°F/Gas 6.

4 Stir the grated cheese into the breadcrumb mixture. Beat the eggs well until frothy and strain into the mixture. Stir together well.

5 Pour the cheese mixture into the pie dish, and bake in the preheated oven for 20 minutes. Serve immediately.

•Version Two is best with ordinary bread, but you could ring the changes in the first one by using more exciting examples – an olive oil one such as ciabatta or focaccia, or even some of the flavoured breads like sundried tomato...

Glamorgan Sausages

SERVES 4

Made from cheese, leeks or onions and breadcrumbs, this is more a savoury, meat-free rissole than a sausage, and it can be cooked in either shape. It is attributed to South Wales, where of course there has always been a strong cheese-cooking tradition (think of *Welsh Rarebit*, see page 60), but similar mixtures exist elsewhere. As a cheese lover, I like these very much, but especially since Franco Taruschio (then of the Walnut Tree in Abergavenny) cooked some superb examples at Turner's one St David's Day. And he's an Italian!

140g (5 oz) Caerphilly cheese
175g (6 oz) fresh white breadcrumbs
55g (2 oz) young leeks or spring onions, finely chopped
1 tbsp chopped fresh chives
½ tsp dried thyme
a pinch of dry English mustard powder
salt and freshly ground black pepper
2 egg yolks
1 egg, beaten
lard for frying

1 Preheat the oven to 200°C/400°F/Gas 6.

2 Grate the cheese and mix in a bowl with 115g (4 oz) of the breadcrumbs. Add the chopped leek or spring onion, chives, thyme, mustard, salt and pepper and egg yolks, and mix well together.

3 Divide the mix into eight, and roll each piece into a sausage shape. Dip the sausages into the beaten egg, and then coat with the remaining breadcrumbs.

4 Fry the sausages in a little lard, until they become golden brown on the outside.

Finish them in the preheated oven for 3-4 minutes.

•If I were going to serve these as a main course, I would accompany them with a rustic, spicy tomato sauce.

•You could also make the mixture into tiny patties and cook to serve as canapés or an *amuse-gueule*.

•As it stands, this is a great dish for vegetarians, but you could cater for meat-eaters too by adding a dice of smoked bacon, ham or cooked sausage to the basic mixture.

Welsh Rarebit

SERVES 4

There is a huge tradition of 'roasting', 'toasting', 'melting', 'grilling' and 'baking' cheese in Britain, and it dates from very early times. The one which has become the most famous and popular is the Welsh version of toasted cheese, or Welsh rarebit. At its simplest, it can be a piece of bread toasted on both sides then topped with a slice of good cheese and grilled, but 'melting' the cheese with other flavourings, then using as a spread on toast, is much more exciting (and traditional). The research for this book was the greatest excuse I could have for ordering Welsh rarebit at each and every eatery I visited. This in my opinion comes very near the top of the pile.

50ml (2 fl oz) double cream
a shake of Worcestershire sauce
1 tbsp beer or ale
2 egg yolks
1 tsp English mustard
4 slices from an uncut wholemeal loaf
225g (8 oz) mature Cheddar, grated

1 Boil the double cream in a medium pan until it starts to thicken. Add the beer and bring back to the boil. Remove from the heat and stir in the mustard, cheese and Worcestershire sauce. Beat in the egg yolks, pour into a bowl, cool and refrigerate. Use the next day.

2 Cut the bread to doorstop size, toast the slices lightly on one side, then spread the other side generously with the Welsh rarebit mixture. Toast under a hot preheated grill until golden and sizzling.

•Serve as a snack or light lunch with a

salad, or cut into small pieces as a traditional savoury. I have to admit my favourite way is late at night, with Marmite or *Piccalilli* (see page 310) spread under the cheese...

•You could use Pommery or grain mustard instead of the French, which gives a different flavour and texture. And recently on *Ready Steady Cook* I was given a Shropshire ale cheese – one that had been soaked in ale – so I had two ingredients ready all in one!

Creamed Mushrooms on Toast

SERVES 4

Grilled or fried mushrooms on toast was one of the most popular – and one of the simplest – of after-dinner savouries. The mushrooms could also be 'devilled' or 'peppered' (kidneys were prepared similarly, see page 159). The finest mushrooms (apart from wild) are the large field mushrooms with the dark gills, and the best way of cooking them is to slow-roast them with garlic, oil and herbs, so that the juices evaporate and concentrate. Using button mushrooms, as here, is more refined, takes much less time, and gives a far nicer colour.

450g (1 lb) small button mushrooms
25g (1 oz) unsalted butter
1 shallot, peeled and finely chopped
150ml (5 fl oz) dry sherry
150ml (5 fl oz) double cream
salt and freshly ground black pepper
1 tbsp chopped fresh chives
4 slices good brown bread, toasted

1 Trim the stalks off the mushrooms (and keep, see below).

2 Melt the butter in a pan, add the mushrooms and sauté them until golden brown.

3 Take the pan off the heat, and add the shallot and dry sherry. Put back on the heat, and boil to reduce the sherry by two-thirds.

4 Add the double cream and bring to the boil. Turn the heat down, and simmer gently until the cream starts to thicken and bind the mushrooms together.

5 Take the pan from the heat and season the mushrooms with salt and pepper. Stir in the chopped chives, spoon over the toast, and serve straightaway.

•Use the stalks, if there are any, for another dish. A duxelles, such as in the *Beef Wellington* recipe (see page 129), would be perfect.

•In the restaurant we might take refinement a step further, and cut circles out of each slice of toast as the base for the mushrooms, as for Scotch Woodcock (see below).

Scotch Woodcock

SERVES 4

This classic after-dinner savoury, the most popular in Victorian times apparently, is basically fancy scrambled eggs on toast. I believe it still appears on the menus of many gentlemen's clubs. The only thing I can see to ally the game bird with the savoury is that both are served on toast. The name of the recipe may also be a snide reference to the parsimony of the Scots (Yorkshiremen stripped of their generosity, as an old joke has it), who might serve scrambled eggs instead of woodcock, the most expensive of the game birds.

4 eggs
4 egg yolks

300ml (10 fl oz) single cream
salt and freshly ground black pepper
55g (2 oz) unsalted butter
4 slices sliced bread
12 anchovy fillets
1 tbsp capers, rinsed
4 fresh parsley leaves

1 Beat the eggs, egg yolks and cream together, then season with salt and pepper. Use 25g (1 oz) of the butter to scramble this mixture.

2 Toast the bread, then butter the slices. Use a round cutter to cut out a large circle from each slice of bread.

3 Load the toast circles with the scrambled eggs. Criss-cross with the anchovy fillets and sprinkle with the capers. Garnish with parsley, and serve immediately.

•Many recipes advocate mashing the anchovy with the butter and spreading it on the toast before topping with the scrambled egg. Or you could use some minced ham mixed with mustard and butter. It's the spiciness you want.

•Don't waste the remnants of buttered toast – eat them!

Angels on Horseback

SERVES 4

Who would have thought this favourite Victorian savoury could be successful, but the sea tang of the oyster with the saltiness of the bacon makes for a perfect marriage. Although a good and tasty mouthful at the end of a meal, the angels (and indeed devils) could also be served as a canapé, a starter or a light lunch. (Incidentally, a scallop cooked in the same way is called an 'archangel'.)

12 rashers streaky bacon
12 large oysters, shelled and cleaned
½ lemon
freshly ground black pepper
a little lard or olive oil, if necessary
4 slices thick white or brown bread
25g (1 oz) unsalted butter
4 sprigs fresh parsley or dill

1 Take the rashers of bacon and stretch out using the back of a large knife so that they are thinner and more elongated than before. Lay out on a chopping board.

2 Meanwhile, take the cleaned oysters, squeeze over the lemon juice and sprinkle on some black pepper.

3 Wrap each oyster with a rasher of bacon and then secure three per person on a wooden skewer (which has been soaked in water if they are to be grilled). Grill until the bacon crisps and the oysters are just cooked. An alternative is to fry them in lard or oil until just cooked.

4 Toast the bread, butter the slices, and cut into your preferred shape. Lay an oyster skewer on each piece of toast and garnish with a sprig of parsley or dill. Serve immediately.

Devils on Horseback

SERVES 4

We have 'angels' and 'devils' because of colour, I presume – the white of the oysters and the black of the prunes. But why 'horseback', I cannot fathom. Whatever the reason for the name, devils on horseback are almost as delicious as angels, the sweetness of the prunes a good contrast with the salty bacon.

12 large prunes
55g (2 oz) unsalted butter
12 rashers streaky bacon
a little lard or olive oil, if necessary
4 slices thick white or brown bread
4 sprigs fresh parsley or dill

1 Stone the prunes, then fry in a frying pan in half the butter. Drain.

2 Stretch the bacon rashers as in the previous recipe, then wrap them round the stoned prunes.

3 Skewer, cook and serve in exactly the same way as the angels on horseback.

3

Fish and Shellfish

For an island nation, we seem to have had a chequered relationship with foods from the sea. From the very earliest days, fish and shellfish had been a hugely important part of the diet of the British: piles of shells have been found in prehistoric sites from the Orkneys to the Channel Islands. By medieval times, fish was as important as bread in the diet, but for a very different reason. The Roman Catholic Church had decreed that three days of each week must be meat free; and during Lent eggs and dairy foods were forbidden as well. This meant that for virtually half the year fish was the only permitted protein (although barnacle geese, puffins and beavers were, curiously, classified as fish). For most people living away from the coasts, this fish had to be preserved in some way – dried, salted, smoked or pickled – and this would undoubtedly have proved a little monotonous after a while. It is probably because of this need to preserve the huge catches of fish that there are so many smoked, pickled and potted fish dishes in the British canon. It may also explain why fish was for so long liked *less* than meat: eating fish was mandatory, while meat was special, for high days and holidays.

As the power of the Church diminished, fish did not need to be eaten so often. Ironically, though, transportation began to improve and fresh fish could at last be enjoyed more widely. With the arrival of faster ships, then the railways, salmon from Scotland, for instance, could be brought down to London fresh rather than smoked. Fish became cheaper as a result and soon became the food of the poor: it was nutritious and didn't require much cooking (many homes did not have any means of cooking food). Stalls selling shellfish – oysters, whelks, cockles – sprang up all over the country. Eels became a favourite dish to buy in London, and salmon was so common that London apprentices were said to have complained at having to eat it several times a week. Fried fish was sold too, often with a potato accompaniment, and this was the forerunner of our very British fish and chips.

Turning full circle, fish and shellfish have recently been looked on as luxury foods, principally due to their scarcity because of pollution and over-fishing. However, things seem to be looking up again, and Rick Stein

has almost single-handedly been responsible for reintroducing us to the joys of fish
cooking at home. I urge you to buy, cook
and enjoy.

Herrings in Mustard and Oatmeal

SERVES 4

Herrings used to be a major part of the
economy of the east coast of Britain,
particularly East Anglia, but sadly they have
been over-fished and stocks are in decline.
Great Yarmouth in Norfolk was the centre
for 'red herrings', whole fish that were
brined and then cold smoked so they turned
from pale to dark red. I went to a herring
fair there once, and I cooked the following
recipe on the sand dunes!

Herrings in Scotland are often served with
a mustard sauce (a reflection of the
Scandinavian influence) or are fried in
oatmeal (*the* Scottish grain). Here I've
combined the two ideas, but I've used Dijon
mustard, as I think English is too strong
(although, interestingly, English mustard is
as Norfolk based as the red herrings above).
Herrings are best in the spring, summer and
autumn.

4 herrings
25g (1 oz) plain flour
salt and freshly ground black pepper
2 eggs, beaten
1 tbsp Dijon mustard
225g (8 oz) fine oatmeal
4 rashers bacon
1 tbsp vegetable oil or 55g (2 oz) lard
25g (1 oz) unsalted butter

1 Make sure the herrings are scaled. Take off the fins and the head of each, then cut down each side of the backbone and pull the backbone out so that the fish is split to look like a kipper. Remove the guts and clean well.

2 Put the flour, seasoned with salt and pepper, the beaten eggs mixed with the mustard, and the oatmeal in three separate flattish plates.

3 Rinse and pat the double fillets dry, then coat them with flour on both sides. Shake off any excess. Dip in the eggs and finally into the fine oatmeal.

4 Fry the bacon in the oil and butter in a frying pan until crisp, and the fat has rendered. Remove from the pan and keep warm.

5 Fry the herrings in the fat remaining in the pan until crisp and golden brown on each side. Cook very gently or the oatmeal will fall off. Drain and serve with a bacon rasher over each double fillet.

Mackerel with Gooseberries and Potatoes

SERVES 4

The French and the English disagree as to who invented the magical marriage of oily mackerel and tart gooseberry. Some say it came in at the time of the Norman Conquest, others that it was a natural combination of May's fat, fresh fish (particularly in Cornwall) and the ripening fruit. No less an expert than M. Escoffier himself, however, suggests that it is English in his recipe for *'Maquereau à l'anglaise'*, poached fish served with a purée of green gooseberries. That's enough proof for me...

4 mackerel
1 tbsp vegetable oil
25g (1 oz) unsalted butter
salt and freshly ground black pepper

Gooseberries and potatoes
25g (1 oz) unsalted butter
55g (2 oz) unrefined caster sugar
25g (1 oz) chopped fresh root ginger
450g (1 lb) gooseberries, trimmed
450g (1 lb) new potatoes, cooked and
  warm
1 tbsp chopped fresh parsley

1 Melt the butter in a pan, add the sugar and then the ginger and gooseberries. Cover with a lid and cook slowly for 5 minutes. Take the lid off and cook gently until all the liquid has evaporated.

2 Meanwhile, fillet the mackerel, then take out the pin bones from each fillet. Cut on each side of where the pin bones are, down to the skin but not through it. Then with your knife and thumb, get hold of the piece of flesh and pull away in one fell swoop taking the bones away (much easier than pulling out individual pin bones using tweezers). Slash the fillets across the skin side at the head end to help even cooking.

3 Heat the oil and butter in a frying pan. Cook the fillets in this until golden brown, about 3-4 minutes, then take out, drain and season.

4 When the gooseberries are cooked, add the new potatoes, heat through briefly, and check the seasoning. Add the chopped parsley, then arrange on hot serving plates. Criss-cross the mackerel fillets over the top and serve.

Jubilee Salmon

SERVES 4

Salmon has always been caught in Britain, primarily in Scottish waters, and there are references to 'kippered salmon' in documents from as early as the mid-fifteenth century. Sadly, there are fewer fish now in the wild, due to pollution and over-fishing. Farmed fish can never be quite the same, although the quality is generally good. If you do come across a wild salmon in the early summer, all you need do is simply poach it; it doesn't need much else doing to it.

I cooked this dish for the actress Liza Goddard when she came on Anglia TV's programme, *Brian Turner's All-Star Cooking*, during the Queen's Jubilee year. Liza was on tour in a play in which she actually played the Queen, and the salmon and asparagus combination was chosen because the Queen had apparently eaten that to celebrate her Silver Jubilee.

4 x 175g (6 oz) salmon steaks, trimmed
  and pin-boned
25g (1 oz) unsalted butter
2 shallots, peeled and finely diced
salt and freshly ground black pepper
12 asparagus spears, trimmed
150ml (5 fl oz) white wine
150ml (5 fl oz) fish stock
4 plum tomatoes, seeded and diced

Herb hollandaise
175g (6 oz) clarified butter (see page 78)
3 egg yolks, lightly beaten
1 tbsp white wine vinegar
2 tbsp lightly chopped fresh tarragon
2 tbsp snipped fresh chives

1 Preheat the oven to 180°C/350°F/Gas 4.

2 Lay the steaks skin side down on the work surface, and make an incision through to the skin from back to belly rather than head to tail. Take care not to cut through the skin. Open up the steak so that the skin is folded in on itself in the middle at the back. You should end up with a rough 'heart shape'.

3 Grease an ovenproof baking dish with

butter, and sprinkle in the finely diced shallot. Add the salmon steaks, and season. Arrange the asparagus spears around them. Add the wine and fish stock, cover with foil and put into the preheated oven for 10 minutes only, no more.

4 Remove from the oven and take out the salmon. Keep this warm. Take out the asparagus spears and trim off the tips. Chop the remainder of the spears finely, and keep both these dice and the tips warm.

5 Meanwhile, dribble a little clarified butter (from the hollandaise ingredients) into a small pan, add the tomatoes and warm through. Season. At the same time, reduce the salmon cooking liquor by two-thirds in another small pan.

6 To make the hollandaise, over a gentle heat, whisk the egg yolks and vinegar in a round-sided pan to a frothy consistency. Do not overcook. Remove from the heat regularly so that the eggs do not overheat and scramble.

7 Take off the heat and, still whisking continuously, slowly drizzle in the remainder of the clarified butter. (If at any time this starts to curdle, add a tsp of cold water to bring it back.) Add the reduced cooking liquor, some seasoning, the chopped herbs and diced asparagus.

8 Arrange the salmon steaks in the middle of individual warm plates and then spoon over the herb hollandaise. Put a tsp or so of tomato dice on the top, and garnish each steak with three asparagus tips. Serve immediately.

•To make clarified butter, put a block of butter in a pan and warm very gently over or beside heat until the milk solids sink to the bottom. Very slowly pour off the clarified golden liquid into another container, leaving the milky residue behind. Clarified butter keeps for ages and you can cook at high temperature with it as it now lacks the solids which burn. (Ghee, the fat used in Indian cooking, is a clarified butter.)

Trout with Almonds

SERVES 4

I think this recipe is probably a French import, but I remember that 90 per cent of the fish courses I served at banquets during my college days and immediately after – in the early 1960s – were *'truite amandine'* or *'truite grenobloise'* (like *meunière*, with capers and lemon segments). The former we took to our hearts, and indeed a good trout needs nothing more than a quick frying in butter, and then the added texture and flavour of some toasted almonds.

4 x 280g (10 oz) trout, scaled, gutted and
   fins removed
25g (1 oz) plain flour
salt and freshly ground black pepper
115g (4 oz) unsalted butter
115g (4 oz) split almonds
juice of 2 lemons
2 tbsp chopped fresh parsley

1 See that the trout are well cleaned, then wash inside and outside and pat dry.

2 Put the flour on a plate, season it, and then dust each fish on both sides, shaking off the excess.

3 Heat half the butter in a frying pan that is large enough to hold at least two fish at a time. Lay the fish carefully in the pan, and cook to golden brown on one side then turn over; turn the heat down, and cook through for 8-10 minutes.

4 Meanwhile, toast the almonds to a light

golden brown in a dry frying pan (watch them), then throw them into the pan with the trout for the last 4 minutes. Take out the trout and place on a hot platter.

5 Add the remaining butter to the cooking pan, and let it colour to a golden brown. Taking the pan off the heat, add the lemon juice and parsley. Bring to the boil, and spoon over the fish to serve.

•I'm sure you already know this, but the correct etiquette when serving trout is to place it on the plate, belly away from the diner (ladies might be offended). I'm not convinced of this, seeing that the heads, eyes and tails are still there, but this is probably why, although it's harder work, fillets of trout are usually served in top restaurants.

Jellied Eels

SERVES 4

Eels, those amazing fish that are born in salt water and travel for some three years back to their fresh home waters in Britain, were once very much more abundant than they are now. They were so prolific, along with mussels and oysters, that they became a popular food with the poor of the East End of London, thus the continuing association of eels with Cockneys! Once street stalls and shops selling pie and mash, eel and mash and jellied eels flourished, but sadly these seem now to be diminishing in number. A shame, because eel is delicious, whether baked, poached, grilled or indeed smoked (the latter one of life's joys).

I went eel fishing once in the Fens when filming the Anglia TV series, *Out to Lunch*. We weren't quite blindfolded, as we were in cars, but our guide took us there and back by the most circuitous route so that we couldn't retrace our steps to where his nets were...

675g (1½lb) fresh eel
2 bay leaves
4 fresh parsley stalks
1 onion, peeled and chopped
6 black peppercorns
salt
150ml (5 fl oz) white wine
300ml (10 fl oz) white wine vinegar
2 tbsp chopped fresh parsley
(lots of parsley is essential)

1 Get the fishmonger to kill, bleed, gut and skin the eel to order, then cut it into 5cm (2 in) lengths.

2 Preheat the oven to 140°C/275°F/Gas 1.

3 Lay the eel pieces in a flat deep pot vertically, then add the bay leaves, parsley stalks, onion, peppercorns and a pinch of salt. Pour in the wine and vinegar, and top up with water to cover well.

4 Put a lid on the pot and put into the preheated oven for 2-3 hours, depending on the thickness of the fish.

5 When the eel is cooked, carefully remove the stock and herbs. Strain the juices, discarding the herbs, then add the chopped parsley. Spoon this back over the eel, and leave to cool overnight, when the juices will set to the characteristic jelly (from the dissolved eel bones).

Grilled Dover Sole

SERVES 4

There are various types of sole, but Dover is the very best.

Sole were once filleted at the table for you in old-fashioned restaurants, and in my capacity as Chairman of the Academy of Culinary Arts, I have been helping to bring back some of those old skills we seem to have lost. In this I am very grateful for the work done by Silvano Giraldin, restaurant manager of the Gavroche, and Sergio Rebecchi of Chez Nico, who have been passing on their vast knowledge to a new generation of chefs and waiters.

4 x 450g (1 lb) whole Dover sole
55g (2 oz) plain flour
salt and freshly ground black pepper
55g (2 oz) unsalted butter, melted
2 lemons, halved

Parsley butter
115g (4 oz) unsalted butter
juice of ½ lemon
1 tbsp chopped fresh parsley

1 Make the parsley butter first. Mix the butter with the lemon juice and parsley, and some salt and pepper. Roll up in dampened greaseproof paper to a sausage shape and put in the freezer until needed. Preheat the grill.

2 To clean the soles, remove the black skin first. Dip the tail into boiling water then, using the back of a knife, scrape from the tail end towards the body to loosen a piece

of the skin. Hold the fish down and grip the skin piece in a cloth. Pull firmly and all will come away. Turn the fish over and carefully remove the scales from the white-skinned side. Remove the head by chopping it off (optional), then cut the side fins away using scissors. Wash and dry well.

3 Season the flour with some salt and pepper and dip the sole, skinned side only, into it. Shake off the excess flour and place on a grilling sheet, floured side up. Brush with melted butter, and grill on one side for about 5-6 minutes. If necessary, turn over, but test for doneness first. Do this by pushing your finger on to the backbone: if the meat gives sufficiently for you to feel bone, the sole is ready.

4 Take the parsley butter from the freezer and using a warm knife, cut into thin slices. Lay two slices on each sole and allow to melt naturally. Serve with half a lemon and new potatoes.

•You probably don't need to know this, but lemon soles, although fine fish, are not true soles – because they are 'left-handed'. True soles like Dovers are dextral or right-handed, because they have both eyes on the right-hand side of their heads. Now you know.

•In restaurants sole are grilled on salamanders, a bottom heat like a barbecue, rather than a top heat. This marks the fish with grid marks, and if you would like to recreate this at home, heat a metal skewer over a flame. Mark the fish before you cook, to scorch the flour.

•You can concoct different savoury butters to accompany grilled fish. Use anchovies, oysters, garlic or tarragon, for instance.

Whitebait

SERVES 4

Whitebait, the fry of herrings and sprats, are said to be so called because they are 'white' and were used as bait to catch larger fish. They once shoaled so prolifically on the coasts and estuaries of Essex and Kent that fisheries grew up around them. They were caught in the Thames as well, and wealthy Londoners used to travel downriver for whitebait dinners at Greenwich. Whitebait used to be a big seller at Simpson's in the Strand, and I think they make a very tasty mid-table nibble for people to share.

The whitebait fishery in Britain is discouraged now because of the effect on mature fish stocks, but frozen fish are brought in from abroad. Let the fish defrost and drain well in a colander before cooking.

450g (1 lb) whitebait
150ml (5 fl oz) milk
85g (3 oz) plain flour
1 tsp cayenne pepper
salt
vegetable oil for deep-frying
1 lemon, quartered

1 Simply put the whitebait into the milk and stir round. Handling carefully, drop them into the flour mixed with the cayenne pepper and salt to taste. Shake off any excess.

2 Heat the oil to 190°C/375°F. Drop the tiny fish into the oil in the fryer, not too many at a time. Fry until golden brown, then strain and drain on kitchen paper.

3 Sprinkle with salt and lemon juice, and serve immediately.

•Don't overcook them: it's very easy to let them frazzle. And don't even *think* of coating them in breadcrumbs: the flour will give you the right texture.

•If you don't like the 'devilled' flavour here, simply leave out the cayenne pepper.

Yorkshire Fishcakes

SERVES 4

There are two different types of fishcake in Yorkshire. One is the traditional one with mashed potato, fish and parsley, which is breadcrumbed or battered then fried. This is known as a 'parsley cake'. What I call a real Yorkshire fishcake is two slices of potato with a piece of fish in the middle. Whenever I travel to Yorkshire by car to work, I call in at Norman's Mermaid fish and chip shop in Morley, my home town, to get a piece of fish, a fishcake or two and a bag of chips.

When I was asked by Tetley to present a high tea at a catering competition, we cooked these fishcakes, followed by custard tarts. All the other chefs there were laughing at our simple menu, but the queue outside our back door for a sample was the largest – and Tetley won as well!

16 x 3mm (⅛in) potato slices
450g (1 lb) fish fillet (cod or haddock)

plain flour for dusting
vegetable oil for deep-frying (lard or
    dripping in the north)

Salt and vinegar batter
175g (6 oz) plain flour
2 tbsp salt
125ml (4 fl oz) water
150ml (5 fl oz) malt vinegar

1 To make the batter, put the flour and salt in a bowl, and make a well in the centre. Add the water and vinegar and whisk until smooth. Leave to rest.

2 Using a 6cm (2½ in) ring, cut the potato slices into even sizes. Cut the fish into thin 55g (2 oz) pieces of a similar size. Dust lightly with flour.

3 Sandwich the pieces of fish between two pieces of potato. Dip the cakes into flour and shake off the excess, then dip into the batter to cover well.

4 Heat the oil in a flat-bottomed pan to about 190°C/375°F. Carefully drop a fish-cake into the hot fat and let it settle to the bottom. Add another couple of fish cakes if there is room. They will rise to the top when hot enough, about 5 minutes. Turn over, then cook for another 5 minutes until brown.

5 Take out and drain well on kitchen paper. They're better left for 5 minutes as they are too hot to eat straightaway, and they do need to drain very well. Serve hot with *Tomato Ketchup* and some *Pease Pudding* if you like (see pages 305 and 207), although I prefer just salt and vinegar.

Fish Pie

SERVES 8

In medieval times, mixtures of fish would have been topped with pastry, both to seal in the flavour, and to serve as a carbo-hydrate accompaniment. Although pastry can of course still be used, we now commonly use the words 'fish pie' to mean fish topped with mashed potato. Comfort food par excellence, but you'll find a few variations here...

225g (8 oz) each of fillets of haddock, white fish, smoked haddock and salmon, skinned
55g (2 oz) unsalted butter
salt and freshly ground black pepper
24 small button onions, peeled

16 small button mushrooms, halved
juice of 1 lemon
75ml (2½ fl oz) dry sherry

Sauce
40g (1½ oz) unsalted butter
40g (1½ oz) plain flour
300ml (10 fl oz) milk
300ml (10 fl oz) double cream
3 tbsp finely chopped spring onion
1 tbsp chopped fresh parsley
a dash of Tabasco sauce

Topping
675g (1 lb) potatoes
55g (2 oz) unsalted butter
1 tbsp vegetable oil
55g (2 oz) clarified butter (see page 78)

1 Cut the fish into evenly sized 2.5cm (1 in) pieces or cubes.

2 Use the butter to grease a large pie dish, and season it with salt and pepper. Preheat the oven to 200°C/400°F/Gas 6.

3 Put the button onions and mushrooms in a saucepan with 150ml (5 fl oz) water. Add the lemon juice, sherry and some salt and pepper. Cover with greaseproof paper, and leave the vegetables over a gentle heat, covered with the lid, so that they steam and cook, about 15 minutes. Strain off the liquid and cool both liquid and vegetables.

4 To make the sauce, melt the butter in a medium pan, add the flour and stir together to make a blond roux. In another pan, bring the milk, cream and the vegetable cooking liquor to the boil together. Slowly add the hot liquid to the roux, stirring, to make a white sauce. Leave to cook for 5 minutes, then add the spring onion, parsley, Tabasco and some salt and pepper if necessary. Put to one side, and cover with clingfilm to prevent a skin forming.

5 Mix the fish with the onions and mushrooms, then pile into the pie dish and season with salt and pepper.

6 For the topping, peel, wash and dry the potatoes and cut into thin slices. Pan-fry the potatoes in the butter and oil to colour nicely. Drain.

7 Pour the sauce over the fish and tap the pie dish to let the air escape. Carefully place the coloured potatoes over the fish in two layers to make a crust, the top layer being nicely presented. It should look like a hotpot topping.

8 Bake in the preheated oven for 25-30

minutes, brushing with the melted clarified butter every now and again during cooking. Serve hot, straight from the oven.

•Or follow all the stages of the recipe, but simply cover the fish and its sauce with mashed potato. It needn't be plain mash: horseradish mash, mustard mash or even bubble and squeak mash would look and taste good.

Mussels with Cider

SERVES 8

We think of mussels as being French (*moules marinières*) or Belgian (*moules et frites*), but of course mussels are found all around the coastlines of Britain, and have been eaten here for centuries. Musselburgh in Scotland was actually named for the famous nearby mussel beds, and there are several soup-stews in traditional Scottish cooking. (Mussels are now farmed in Scotland and Ireland, on ropes.) Mussels feature in Welsh and Irish cooking as well – think of Molly Malone plying her live 'cockles and mussels' through the Dublin streets.

Instead of the French wine, I have used our

English cider here, along with apples, and the flavours are good.

2.25 litres (4 pints) mussels
2 shallots, peeled and chopped
2 apples, cored and finely diced
300ml (10 fl oz) dry cider
2 tbsp chopped fresh parsley
150ml (5 fl oz) double cream
juice of ½ lemon
25g (1 oz) unsalted butter
salt and freshly ground black pepper

1 Clean the mussels well, removing the beards, and discard any that are cracked, or remain open after you tap them sharply against the edge of the sink. Put into a large heavy-bottomed pan.

2 Add the chopped shallot, the apple dice, cider and half the chopped parsley. Cover with a lid. Cook over a fierce heat until all the mussels have opened, about 6-7 minutes.

3 Lift the mussels out, using a spider sieve, into a colander over a bowl. Strain the cooking liquor into a clean bowl and allow to stand for 5 minutes to allow any sand to sink to the bottom. Discard the vegetables.

4 Carefully strain the liquor into a clean pan, taking care not to disturb any sand at the bottom. Add any liquor from below the mussels as well.

5 Add the cream and lemon juice to the liquor, and boil to reduce by half. Add the butter and remaining parsley, and check the seasoning.

6 Meanwhile, discard any mussels that remain closed. (If in doubt, throw 'em out, they're really quite cheap.) Divide them between eight soup plates, pour the sauce over and serve immediately.

Dressed Crab

SERVES 4

I love crab, and still remember the crab paste we used to have in Yorkshire as kids (once a speciality of Scarborough, I believe). I've been fortunate enough to have worked in three British crab areas. In Cromer, Norfolk, where the crabs are very small but sweet, I met Richard David who catches them at sea and sells them on the High Street. I've also cooked and tasted crab in Whitby, further north, where they are bigger – and indeed they seem to get bigger the further north you go, particularly in Scotland. However, perhaps to gainsay that, I've caught and eaten crab in Guernsey (where they're called 'shankers'), and there they are quite massive.

Most crabs are dressed in their shells, but I think there is complication enough already in getting all the meat out without worrying about keeping the shells whole. I just serve the white and dark meat separately in bowls, and use the shells for quite a different purpose (see page 97).

1 x 1.8kg (4 lb) live male crab
4.5 litres (7½ pints) water
175g (6 oz) salt

To dress the crab
juice of 1 lemon
Tabasco sauce to taste
Worcestershire sauce to taste
55g (2 oz) fresh white breadcrumbs
salt and freshly ground black pepper
4 hard-boiled eggs, shelled
2 tbsp chopped fresh parsley
1 small onion, peeled and finely chopped

1 Bring the salted water up to the boil, plunge in the crab, bring back to the boil and simmer for 25 minutes. Then take off the heat and allow the crab to cool in the liquor. Take out, drain, and put into the fridge. Alternatively, you can buy a fresh cooked

crab from a reputable fishmonger.

2 Twist off the legs and claws, and break each joint so that it is easier to remove the meat. Using a small hammer to tap and crack open the pieces, and a skewer, push all the pieces of white meat out into a bowl. The claws contain the nicest, sweetest and moistest meat, but this needs careful checking for any bones.

3 Next take the body in one hand, then, using a kitchen knife, insert and twist to remove the central case of the body that held the legs and claws. Pull this free then remove the ring of 'dead men's fingers' and throw away. This will reveal the brown crabmeat. Using a spoon remove this from the shell and put into another bowl.

4 Break the brown meat up, adding the lemon juice, Tabasco and Worcestershire sauces to taste, and enough breadcrumbs to form a paste which is not too soft. Season to taste with salt and pepper.

5 Pass the boiled eggs through a sieve, add the parsley and onion, and mix well together.

6 Put the brown meat into a shallow bowl with the egg mixture scattered around the edge to decorate.

7 Serve the white meat in a separate bowl, perhaps with a lemon mayonnaise, brown bread and butter, and even a tomato salad for perfection.

•You may think I have forgotten to season the white meat. But I don't think it needs it. Try it and see.

•Don't waste your time keeping the shells for presentation. Break them up with the claws, using a hammer, and put them in a pot with fish stock, garlic, tomatoes and other vegetable flavourings to make a strong stock. Take the shells out and put some rice in. Pound the shells, and return to the pan until the rice is cooked. Press everything through a fine sieve, squeezing to get as much flavour out as possible. Add double cream and brandy to taste, and you will have a wonderful crab soup.

Lobster with Dill, Tomato and Mustard

SERVES 4

Lobsters have always been highly rated and highly priced, and those of Scotland are said to be the best in Britain, growing sweet in the cold waters of the north. But I have eaten lobsters much further south, in the Channel Islands, and in Alderney, so legend has it, the lobster population flourished and grew fat on the bodies of slave labourers thrown into the sea around the island during the German occupation in the 1940s...

This recipe is similar to a Scottish one, and to many that became popular in Victorian times in gentlemen's clubs. It's my 'almost Thermidor'. A lobster per person is a large main course, but I think if you're pampering yourself, you don't want half measures. However, as a first course, two lobsters between four would be sufficient.

4 x 450g (1 lb) live lobsters (approx. weight)
55g (2 oz) unsalted butter

1 shallot, peeled and chopped
150ml (5 fl oz) fish stock
150ml (5 fl oz) white wine
300ml (10 fl oz) double cream
4 tbsp crème fraîche
1 tbsp Dijon mustard
salt and freshly ground black pepper
2 tbsp chopped fresh dill
4 tomatoes, finely diced
2 egg yolks
55g (2 oz) Parmesan, freshly grated

1 Cook the lobsters by plunging in boiling water and boiling for 4 minutes, then take out and leave to cool.

2 Split the carcass in half lengthways. Take out the body meat carefully and put to one side. Break off the claws, and separate into the three different joints, removing the cartilage from the middle of the pincer. Gently tap the joints with the back of a large knife and take out the meat. Keep separate. Discard the intestinal tract from the body then cut the body meat into nice-sized pieces.

3 Preheat the oven to 160°C/325°F/Gas 3. Wash and clean four of the half shells, and put them in the oven to warm through.

4 Meanwhile, melt half the butter in a pan,

and sweat off the shallot, not allowing it to colour. Add the fish stock and white wine and reduce by two-thirds. Add the double cream, boil and reduce by half until thickened. Remove from the heat, add the crème fraîche and mustard, mix in and season.

5 Heat the sauce gently then add the lobster meat except for the claws. Heat through gently but well. Dab the claw meat with the remaining butter and heat for a few minutes in the low oven.

6 Add the chopped dill and tomato dice to the sauce, then beat in the egg yolks. Pour this mixture evenly into the four warm half lobster shells.

7 Lay the meat from a claw on top of each mounded half lobster, sprinkle with the Parmesan, colour under the preheated grill and serve.

•If there are eggs in the tail of a female, or a greenish sac in the head (the tomalley), make sure you use these in the sauce.

•Break up the spare half shells, put into a small but tall saucepan, and add some unsalted butter. Leave to stew slowly on the side of the stove. The butter will turn red and taste incredibly of lobster. Strain. You can chill this flavoured butter, or freeze it, to use in sauces.

Salad of Scallops with Bacon

SERVES 4

The combination of scallops and bacon crops up in Scottish, English and Manx cooking, one of those wonderful anomalies of flavour balance, which is similar to oysters and bacon (see page 66) and the Welsh trout cooked with bacon. I've taken it a little into the present time by presenting it in a salad.

Scallops are one of our most delicious shellfish, native to the cold waters of western Scotland and around the Isle of Man (where there has apparently been a scallop fishery for some 3,000 years). Giant or king scallops are the largest, the queens or queenies being much smaller (and, if used instead, you will need six to seven – or even more – instead of three per person).

12 large scallops in the shell
5 tbsp olive oil
salt and freshly ground black pepper

101

6 rashers smoked back bacon
6 spring onions, chopped
1 tbsp grain mustard
2 tbsp white wine vinegar
2 tbsp groundnut oil
1 tbsp each of chopped fresh parsley,
   chives and chervil

To serve
mixed salad leaves (more or less,
   depending on whether for a starter or
   main course)

1 Trim the scallops, using the white muscle meat only for this dish.

2 Heat 1 tbsp of the olive oil in a solid flat-bottomed frying pan, and sear the scallops until golden brown, a minute or two only. Turn over just to sear, season and then take out and keep warm.

3 Meanwhile, trim the bacon and cut into thin strips. Sauté and colour these in the frying pan that the scallops were cooked in. Add the chopped spring onion, and sauté until coloured, and then put both bacon and onion into a large bowl.

4 Mix the mustard and vinegar well in a bowl or jar, then add the remaining olive oil, the groundnut oil, herbs and some seasoning. Take some of the dressing and toss with the salad leaves then lay these in the middle of four plates.

5 Add the remaining dressing to the bacon and onion. Balance the three scallops per person on each mound of salad leaves, and then spoon the bacon, onion and dressing over and around.

Potted Shrimps

SERVES 4

Shrimp teas were traditional in the north of England, and potted shrimps became a popular feature of afternoon tea in the late eighteenth century. The shrimp industry in Britain centres on the dangerous shifting sands and shallow waters of Morecambe Bay in Lancashire, where tractors now carry the nets instead of horses. Brown cold-water shrimps, found along many coasts in northern Europe, are very small (which makes them difficult to shell), but taste wonderful. The shelled shrimps widely available now come mostly from Holland, and I urge you to buy those you can shell yourself. The shells will make a fantastic stock. Or, if you can't be bothered with shelling, simply blend the fish, shells and all, to make a great paste for spreading on toast.

Fish or meat has been preserved in butter like this since at least the sixteenth century.

140g (5 oz) clarified butter (see page 78)
350g (12 oz) peeled cooked brown
    shrimps
a pinch of ground mace
1 tsp anchovy essence
a pinch of cayenne pepper
lemon juice (optional)

1 Preheat the oven to 150°C/300°F/Gas 2.

2 Melt the clarified butter, then take out just less than half and put to one side. Add the brown shrimps to the bulk of the butter in the pan, and season with the mace, anchovy essence and cayenne pepper. You must taste at this stage and if you are unhappy with the balance, add the lemon juice.

3 Now lift the shrimps out using a slotted spoon, and divide between four ramekins or nice oven-to-table dishes.

4 Pour the seasoned butter equally over the shrimps and put the ramekins into a bain-marie (a roasting tray) with warm water. Put this into the preheated oven and cook for 30 minutes. Remove the ramekins from the oven and the tray, and tap the ramekins gently on a carefully folded cloth to get rid of any air bubbles in the mix.

5 Melt the remaining clarified butter and pour gently over the top of the mixture, then leave to cool and set.

Kedgeree

SERVES 4

Although thought of as a quintessentially English dish, kedgeree originated in India during the days of the Raj (as did *Mulligatawny Soup*, see page 30). The original *'khichri'* was a vegetarian combination of rice and lentils. It was thought to be the British Army in India who adapted it to be a rice-only breakfast dish, and who added bits of dried or salted fish. Smoked haddock is the most common fish used now (salmon too), and it's on the menu as such at our Foxtrot Oscar restaurants, very popular with old colonials and old public schoolboys – and, much to my surprise, we sell a lot to young people as well.

550g (1¼ lb) smoked haddock fillet
600ml (1 pint) fish stock
1 bay leaf
juice of 1 lemon
salt and freshly ground black pepper
25g (1 oz) unsalted butter
1 onion, peeled and finely chopped
225g (8 oz) long-grain rice
1 tsp curry powder
a pinch of cayenne pepper
a pinch of freshly grated nutmeg
a pinch of saffron strands (optional)
4 hard-boiled eggs, shelled
1 tbsp chopped fresh coriander

1 Preheat the oven to 180°C/350°F/Gas 4.

2 Make sure the haddock fillet is skinned and boned totally. Put into a large oven-proof dish. Bring the fish stock to the boil, and pour over the fish. Add the bay leaf and lemon juice, and season well. Cook covered in the preheated oven for 5 minutes until just cooked. Strain off the stock.

3 Meanwhile, melt the butter in a sauce-pan, add the onion and sweat without colouring for a few minutes until soft. Add the rice and stir, then cook until the rice is completely coated with butter. Add the spices.

4 Pour in the strained fish stock topped up with enough water to make twice the volume of the rice. Cover with buttered greaseproof paper and cook in the pre-heated oven as above for 18 minutes.

5 Take out of the oven, leave to sit for 2 minutes, and then stir with a fork.

6 Cut the eggs into big chunks, add half to the rice and stir in. Check the seasoning of the rice, then pour into a warmed serving bowl. Flake the smoked haddock over the top, sprinkle with the rest of the eggs and coriander and serve.

Prawn Cocktail

SERVES 4

No-one seems to be quite sure where and when the infamous prawn cocktail originated, but it appeared on restaurant menus in Britain throughout the 1960s, and can still be found today. It may be an American idea. A combination of shredded lettuce, prawns and, usually, a bottled mayo-based sauce, it has been much maligned, but in actual fact when made correctly, can be wonderful. Marco Pierre White even included it on his Mirabelle menu!

350g (12 oz) shelled prawns
1 little gem lettuce
1 tbsp Dijon mustard
1 tbsp white wine vinegar
4 tbsp olive oil
salt and freshly ground black pepper
2 tbsp finely chopped cucumber

Sauce
6 tbsp mayonnaise
2 tbsp *Tomato Ketchup* (see page 305)
1 tbsp double cream
1 tsp each of brandy and creamed horseradish
juice of ½ lemon
4 drops Tabasco sauce

To garnish
2 tomatoes, seeded and finely diced
1 shallot, peeled and finely chopped
1 tbsp chopped fresh chives

1 Put the prawns into a bowl. Finely shred the lettuce.

2 Make a vinaigrette with the mustard, vinegar and oil. Season with salt and pepper.

3 Make the sauce by mixing the mayonnaise with the ketchup and cream, then stir in the brandy, horseradish, lemon juice and Tabasco. Check the seasoning.

4 Mix the prawns with 1 tbsp of the sauce and 1 tbsp of the vinaigrette.

5 Mix the shredded lettuce with the cucumber, add the remaining vinaigrette and season.

6 Put the lettuce into four glasses, with the prawns on top. Cover lightly with the rest of the sauce.

7 Mix the tomatoes, shallot and chives, sprinkle over the sauce and serve.

4

Meat and Offal

In the very earliest of times, meat and offal would have been cooked beside or on the fire. Once metal cooking pots were invented, meat could be boiled or stewed in water. Most meat eaten was actually 'game' – even cattle, pigs, sheep and goats were animals of the wild until they were domesticated. Cows, sheep and goats could be milked, so had a dual purpose, while pigs, because they could forage for themselves and be fed on scraps, were perhaps most commonly attached to households large and small.

It was not until the seventeenth century that crops were introduced specifically to feed animals during winter. Before then animals would have been slaughtered during the autumn. The offal would have been cooked then and there, or preserved by salting, drying or smoking. Nowadays we seem only to use the superior 'organ' meats, such as liver, kidneys and sweetbreads, disliking the lesser offal as 'poverty food' perhaps.

The meat of the slaughtered beasts would have been preserved too, by salting principally, but 'corning' was popular in Ireland. Fresh meat was eaten of course, but until the problem of over-wintering was solved it would have been largely seasonal. The tender cuts would have spit-roasted beside the fire (our current 'roasting' in an enclosed space is actually baking), and tougher cuts would have been boiled, often in a pottage, or wrapped in a cloth or a suet casing as a pudding. Once ovens developed, other meat-cooking techniques could evolve, such as braising and baking in or under pastry. Britain was once famous for its meat pies, and we have quite a few still – steak and kidney, veal and ham, the Scottish mutton pie, and Cornish pasties.

Why Britain became so renowned for its roast meats is not easily explained. But, despite increasing French culinary influences throughout the centuries, the love of roast meats, plainly served and sauced, did not diminish. Some say it was because the quality of the meat was so good. In France, animals were worked until old, then slaughtered; the flesh would be tougher and riper, so needed fancy flavourings and longer, more complicated cooking to render it palatable. In Britain, animals were reared specifically for the table, so therefore could be roasted much more successfully.

Why the British still love meat so much is just as unclear, but 'meat and two veg' is almost mandatory, at least for Sunday lunch.

Roast Beef and Yorkshire Pudding

SERVES 8-10

Whatever the reason for the undeniable quality of our beef, Britain wouldn't be so great without its roast beef and Yorkshire pudding. I remember we cooked 25-pound sirloins on the bone at Simpson's in the Strand, and then we took them into the dining room to be carved in front of the guests.

Batter puddings are traditional all over the British Isles, and Yorkshire pudding is the most famous, originally cooked in the tray of dripping under the meat as it turned on the spit. Why it became so associated with Yorkshire, I don't know. Perhaps it was because of the renowned meanness of my fellow countrymen: the pudding was served first, before the meat, in order to fill people up so that they would then eat less meat! To me its main purpose is to soak up the meat juices and the gravy.

1 x 4.5kg (10 lb) rib of beef (5 ribs)
salt and freshly ground black pepper

Yorkshire pudding
1 large cup plain flour
a pinch of salt
1 large cup eggs
1 large cup milk and water mixed
1 tbsp malt vinegar

1 For the Yorkshire pudding batter, sift the flour and salt into a large bowl. Add the eggs and beat well with half the liquid until all the lumps have disappeared. Add the rest of the liquid and the vinegar, and allow to stand.

2 Meanwhile, preheat the oven to 220°C/425°F/Gas 7.

3 Prepare the meat by cutting down the backbone towards the rib bones with the knife angled towards the backbone. Take a chopper and then break the backbones near the bottom of the cut (this is called chining). Lift up the fat from the back and take out the rubbery sinew. Tie the beef with string.

4 Put the joint into a roasting tray and season well. Roast in the preheated oven for

30 minutes and then reduce the heat to 190°C/375°F/Gas 5 for a further 1½ hours. This will give you blood-red beef in the middle. The way to check this is by using a meat thermometer to test to 55C/130F or, as I prefer, by plunging a metal skewer through the middle of the beef, holding it there for 10 seconds and then running it either across the wrist or under the bottom lip. If the skewer is cold the meat is not ready: if warm, it's medium; and if hot, then the meat is well done.

5 When cooked, put the meat in a warm place to rest for 20-30 minutes before carving and serving. Meanwhile, increase the oven temperature again to 200°C/400°F/Gas 6.

6 Heat some of the excess dripping from the roast in a suitably sized ovenproof pan or roasting tray. Whisk up the Yorkshire pudding batter, then pour into the tray and immediately place in the oven. Close the door quickly, and bake for 25 minutes. Turn the pan round and cook on for another 10 minutes.

7 Meanwhile, carve and portion the beef on to hot plates, and make a gravy using the juices left in the roasting tray (see the *Roast Chicken* recipe on page 165). As soon as the

Yorkshire pudding is ready, serve with mustard and *Horseradish Sauce* (see page 327), or indeed some horseradish mustard.

•The bigger the joint, the better the meat, and it should always be cooked on the bone. The meat should have a good covering of fat, be dark red in colour (which shows it has been hung properly), and have a good marbling of fat throughout.

•Sprinkling some English mustard powder over the top of the meat halfway through its cooking gives a nice heat.

•This Yorkshire pudding recipe works not by weight, but by volume. Use any size of cup, but measure each ingredient with the same cup. I'm not sure why the vinegar is there, but that's what my gran did. It seems to work, so why change it?

•Yorkshire pudding is very versatile. It can be eaten by itself, with onions and gravy, or can be used in a sweet context as well – not surprising, as the batter is virtually the same as that for popovers and pancakes. In Yorkshire we eat it with sugar and jam, and that's *after* the pudding and the meat!

Toad in the Hole

SERVES 4

Many traditional British batter puddings included some meat, a convenient way of stretching small amounts of protein. Toad in the hole is usually now made with sausages – the Yorkshire beef ones are particularly good – but originally it would have been pieces of leftover meat or, rather posher, pieces of raw rump or fillet steak, or lamb chops.

  Yorkshire pudding batter (see page 116)
  55g (2 oz) beef dripping or lard
  12 pork sausages

1 Make the batter as described on page 116, and leave to rest.

2 Preheat the oven to 200°C/400°F/Gas 6.

3 Heat the dripping or lard in a suitably sized ovenproof pan or roasting tray, and colour the sausages on top of the stove. Put the pan into the preheated oven and cook for 10 minutes.

4 Whisk up the batter, and then immediately pour into the tray and return to the oven. Close the door quickly, and bake for 25 minutes. Turn the pan round and cook on for another 10 minutes. Serve immediately.

Boiled Silverside of Beef and Dumplings

SERVES 4-6

Centuries ago, because animals could not be over-wintered, most (apart from breeding stock) were killed in the autumn and the meat was salted to preserve it. Salted meat (except pork) cannot be roasted, grilled or fried, so it had to be boiled, thus the many traditional boiled meat recipes in the British canon. (And indeed in many other European cuisines – think of the French *pot au feu*, the Italian *bollito misto* and the Swiss *Berner Platte*.) Boiled meat has a texture and flavour that is its own, and we shouldn't dismiss it as less interesting than roast. Fresh meat can be used instead of salt.

And the suet dumplings are uniquely British. Apparently they were invented in

Norfolk in the sixteenth century, probably evolving from the use of suet crust as the container for boiled meats.

1 x 1.3-1.8kg (3-4 lb) piece of salted silverside
2 large onions, peeled
1 leek
2 large carrots
6 black peppercorns
1 bay leaf
2 blades of mace

Vegetables
225g (8 oz) small carrots
225g (8 oz) small onions
450g (1 lb) small leeks (about 4)
225g (8 oz) swede
450g (1 lb) small new potatoes

Dumplings
175g (6 oz) plain flour
1½ tsp baking powder
a pinch of salt
85g (3 oz) chopped beef suet
2 tsp creamed horseradish
water

1 Check with your butcher whether the silverside needs to be soaked: it's often not really necessary these days. Cover the silverside with water, bring to the boil, then

refresh in cold water.

2 Put the meat into a clean pan with the onions, leek, carrots, peppercorns, bay leaf and mace. Bring to the boil, then turn the heat down, and simmer very gently for about 2½-3 hours. Check doneness by strongly ramming a roasting fork into the joint and then carefully lifting up. When done, the meat will slip off the fork easily.

3 Prepare the vegetables and trim into manageable sized pieces. Wrap each type of vegetable in separate cloths and tie with string. About half an hour from the end of cooking, drop all the vegetables into the stock with the meat. They will cook at different rates, usually the potatoes first, then the carrots, swede, onion and then the leeks. Take these out and keep warm.

4 To make the dumplings, mix the flour, baking powder and salt together, then rub in the suet. Mix with the horseradish and enough water to make the mixture come together to a soft, sticky dough.

5 Take some of the liquor out of the silverside pan, strain and bring to the boil in a clean pan. Take 1 tbsp of the dumpling mixture at a time and drop carefully into the liquor. They will swell, so don't put too

many in at once. While these are cooking, take the beef out of its liquor and leave to rest, keeping it warm.

6 Serve in large deep bowls. Put the vegetables in first, then slice the beef and lay around the vegetables. Drain the dumplings well, and put on top of the dish. Check the seasoning of the stock, then strain some over each dish, and serve.

•Boiled beef with carrots is the most famed of the boiled beef dishes, but there is no reason why other root vegetables should not be used instead of or as well as.

•You could vary the dumplings. You could add chopped fresh herbs – parsley is very traditional – or even a fried croûton in the middle of the dumpling, which adds a crisp texture.

•Serve with grated fresh horseradish or a horseradish cream.

•There should be plenty of meat left over for sandwiches.

Steak and Kidney Pudding

SERVES 4

The combination of steak and kidney, although it seems as if it might always have existed, was only recorded in a recipe as late as the mid-nineteenth century. Steak puddings, however, had been made for centuries before, bringing together the suet crust used in the early boiled puddings, and the beef for which England in particular was so famous.

A good steak and kidney pudding is a wonderfully traditional British dish, brought to the table steaming in its bowl, often with a clean white napkin wrapped around it. It's a great favourite in gentlemen's clubs, and I remember we made many at Simpson's in the Strand. There, for some reason, they never served the pastry from inside the bowl, which I think is the most flavoursome, imbued with all the juices of the meats. Small individual puddings are now made – I've seen versions in foil, sold in Blackpool's fish and chip shops – and at one time I created a baked version for Beefeater Restaurants (which worked, not becoming too crusty, so long as it wasn't cooked for too long).

25g (1 oz) beef dripping
675g (1½ lb) topside of beef, trimmed and cut into 2.5cm (1 in) cubes
350g (12 oz) ox kidney, trimmed and cut into 2.5cm (1 in) cubes
1 large onion, peeled and finely chopped
350g (12 oz) field mushrooms, peeled and cut into 5mm (¼ in) strips
25g (1 oz) plain flour
300ml (10 fl oz) meat stock
150ml (5 fl oz) red wine
1 tbsp Worcestershire sauce
salt and freshly ground black pepper
unsalted butter for greasing
1 tbsp mixed chopped fresh parsley and thyme

Suet pastry
280g (10 oz) self-raising flour
½ tsp baking powder
a pinch of salt
140g (5 oz) chopped beef suet
about 2-3 tbsp iced water
55g (2 oz) unsalted butter

1 Preheat the oven to 180°C/350°F/Gas 4.

2 Heat the dripping in a casserole, add the beef and kidney and colour on all sides. Add

123

the onion and mushroom strips, and cook for 2 minutes. Sprinkle with the plain flour, take off the heat and mix the stock, wine and Worcestershire sauce in well. Season with salt and pepper, then put into the preheated oven, and cook for 1 hour. Remove the casserole from the oven and allow to cool.

3 To make the pastry, put the self-raising flour, baking powder and salt into a bowl and mix. Rub in the suet, then add enough iced water to bind to a fairly soft, pliable dough. Leave to rest for about 20 minutes.

4 Butter a 1.2 litre (2 pint) pudding basin well, and have ready a steamer large enough to hold it, or a large saucepan with a stand in it on which the bowl can sit. Cut a circle of greaseproof paper, larger than the circumference of the top of the bowl. Make a couple of pleats in this, and grease the pleated side.

5 Divide the pastry into three-quarters, and one-quarter. Take the larger piece and roll it out to a circle to line the basin, with 1cm (½ in) extra hanging over the edge. Gently line the pudding basin.

6 Mix the herbs into the meat mixture, and pour this mixture into the bowl. Wet the lip of the pastry with water, then roll the remaining pastry out to cover the top. Place on top of the basin, and press down well to seal.

7 Put the greaseproof paper, pleated and greased side down, over the pudding. This pleat allows the pudding to expand. Tie the paper on round the top of the basin, under the lip, with string, and make a handle as well, so that you can lift it in and out easily.

8 Put the pudding in the top of the steamer over boiling water or on the stand in the saucepan, with enough boiling water to come halfway up the pudding. Cover; bring to the boil and cook for 2 hours. Check the water level occasionally.

9 Serve the pudding from the bowl. Slice the top off, lift it off, and spoon out the meat and juices. Serve each person a bit of the top and some of the juicy pastry from the sides.

Beef Olives

SERVES 4

The idea of olives – a flavourful filling encased in a thin slice of meat, and braised – has been around for a long time in Britain. Apparently the veal version was a seventeenth-century variant on the much older beef or mutton olives, which were once called 'allowes' (possibly how the name 'olives' evolved). The idea is not uniquely British, though: think of the French *paupiettes* and the Italian *involtini* or *bocconcini*.

This was one of the first dishes I learned to cook at college, useful because it embodies all of the basic principles of stewing and braising. I've adapted it, though, principally in the sauce: incorporating the braised sieved vegetables into the sauce gives extra flavour, thickness and richness. So serve with separately cooked vegetables, but if you wanted to be more sophisticated, you could do a dice of carrots and add them to the sauce at the last minute to cook and heat through.

4 x 175g (6 oz) slices topside beef
25g (1 oz) unsalted butter

55g (2 oz) fresh breadcrumbs
½ tsp chopped fresh thyme
1 tsp chopped fresh parsley
1 tbsp chopped cooked bacon
1 egg
salt and freshly ground black pepper
55g (2 oz) beef dripping
1 onion, peeled and finely chopped
1 carrot, peeled and finely chopped
1 garlic clove, peeled and crushed
1 tbsp tomato purée
150ml (5 fl oz) red wine
850ml (1½ pints) brown meat stock

1 Tap the slices of topside out evenly between two layers of plastic or clingfilm to make them thinner. Be careful not to tear them.

2 Melt the butter, then add the breadcrumbs, herbs and bacon. Stir in the egg and some salt and pepper, and mix together well. Smear equal parts of this stuffing on to each tapped-out piece of meat, season again and roll up into a cylinder shape. Tie with thin string to hold together, to look like a mini Swiss roll.

3 Meanwhile, preheat the oven to 160°C/325°F/Gas 3.

4 Heat the dripping in a casserole, and seal

and colour the olives. Remove from the casserole. Add the chopped vegetables to the hot fat and colour lightly, followed by the garlic and then the tomato puree. Stir in the red wine and boil to reduce by half.

5 Lay the olives in the casserole, and add the brown stock. Stir, then bring to the boil. Cover with greaseproof paper and a lid, then put into the preheated oven and cook for 1-1½ hours.

6 Remove the olives from the sauce and keep warm. Reduce the sauce a little over a high heat, then push through a sieve. Check the seasoning and consistency. Remove the string carefully from the olives, then pour the sauce over them and serve. Delicious with mashed potato.

•Instead of bacon, you could use parma ham in the filling or, to be really outrageous, you could use haggis by itself.

Beef Wellington

SERVES 4

I have been unable to discover the origins of this dish, but it was named for the first Duke of Wellington, who defeated Napoleon at Waterloo in 1815. He was no gourmet, it's said, but the pastry-encased fillet, glazed and shiny brown, looks rather like the leather boot that also came to be associated with him. It is most similar in concept, actually, to the Russian dish, *coulibiac*, in that a prime piece of protein is encased in several layers before being baked or roasted.

675g (1½ lb) beef fillet, a piece cut from the centre of the fillet
1 tbsp vegetable oil
salt and freshly ground black pepper
25g (1 oz) unsalted butter
1 shallot, peeled and chopped
55g (2 oz) cooked ham, diced
350g (12 oz) button mushrooms, minced
115g (4 oz) meat pâté or terrine
1 tbsp chopped fresh parsley
6 large, about 25cm (10 in) pancakes (see page 132)

2 eggs, beaten with a little water
450g (1 lb) puff pastry

1 Tie the fillet with butcher's string to keep a nice round shape.

2 Heat the oil in a frying pan. Seal the beef fillet and colour well on all sides. Leave to cool, then remove the strings and season with salt and pepper.

3 Meanwhile, melt the butter and sweat the shallot without colouring. Add the ham and minced button mushrooms and cook, stirring regularly, until all the liquor has evaporated and the mushrooms are quite dry. Season and leave to cool (this is now what is called a duxelles).

4 Mix the pâté and parsley with the mushrooms. Smear half of this mixture evenly over the top of the beef fillet.

5 Lay the pancakes out to make a 'sheet' of pancakes, side by side and overlapping. Lift the fillet carefully on to the centre of the pancake sheet, upside down so that the 'bare' side is uppermost. Smear the exposed side with the remaining mushroom mixture so that it is now completely covered with the duxelles. Brush the edges of the pancakes with the egg wash and carefully fold these over to completely seal the beef in the pancakes.

6 Roll out the pastry to about 3mm (⅛in) thick. Trim the pastry into an even oblong just enough to fold over the beef. Brush the edges of the puff pastry with the egg wash. Lay the pancake-covered beef in the centre, and fold the edges of the pastry in and over to make a neat parcel. Turn over so that the joins are underneath. Reshape if necessary, and cut a cylindrical hole in the top to allow the steam to escape. Egg wash and decorate if wanted, then leave to rest for 30 minutes.

7 Preheat the oven to 200°C/400°F/Gas 6.

8 Egg wash the pastry again, then bake the Wellington in the preheated oven for 25 minutes. Turn the oven down to 160°C/325°F/Gas 3 and cook for another 10-15 minutes until the pastry is brown and the meat inside is nicely rare. Cover with foil if the pastry is getting too brown.

9 Leave to rest for about 15 minutes, just like any other roast meat. One of the best ways to test whether the meat is done is to stick a skewer in the middle, count to ten, and then run the skewer along your bottom lip. You'll feel a variance in temperature, the middle part being the coolest. You should feel hot, hot, cool, cool, hot, hot.

10 When slicing, take off the end bits first, as they will be well done. Serve with a Madeira sauce (see page 330).

•The pancakes and pâté/duxelles layers here are vital to prevent the juices of the fillet running into the pastry.

•You could use brioche pastry instead of puff, but that is considerably more complicated as you have to make it from scratch.

•Other ingredients could be used to encase the fillet inside the pastry, such as sun-dried tomato paste or olive paste, or spinach, but then it would no longer strictly be a Wellington.

•Everyone has a pancake recipe, but if you don't, use the Yorkshire pudding recipe on page 114 to make thin pancakes.

Cornish Pasties

MAKES 12

Variations of this idea – ingredients wrapped in pastry to make individual pies – occur all over Europe, but perhaps the nearest to the most famous one, that of Cornwall, are the Forfar Bridie, from the east of Scotland, and the Lancashire Foot. There are all sorts of legends surrounding the quintessential pasty: it is real only if it is dropped down a Cornish tin mine and the pastry doesn't break; that it is unlucky to take a pasty aboard a ship. In Cornwall, the pasty is occasionally called Tiddy Oggy (a local name for potato).

The basic recipe can also be varied in a number of ways. You could use any meat as a filling, and you could use vegetables alone (common when money for the costly meat was scarce). Whatever and however, the pasty is the ultimate portable food, as handy now for a picnic as it once was for the miner to take into the bowels of the earth or the farmer into the field.

Shortcrust pastry
450g (1 lb) plain flour

a pinch of salt
225g (8 oz) lard
55g (2 oz) butter
approx. 150m (5 fl oz) water
2 eggs, beaten with a little water for egg
  wash

Filling
450g (1 lb) topside beef
1 medium onion
225g (8 oz) potatoes
55g (2 oz) carrots
55g (2 oz) turnip
salt and freshly ground black pepper
1 tbsp chopped parsley
Worcestershire sauce
Tabasco sauce

1 To make the pastry, sift the flour and salt into a bowl. Chop the lard and butter straight from the fridge into small cubes, then rub into the flour until like breadcrumbs. Add enough water to make the ingredients come together to a dough, then clingfilm and rest for 30 minutes.

2 Preheat the oven to 200°C/400°F/Gas 6.

3 To make the filling, trim the meat of all fat and gristle, cut into small dice then put into a bowl. Peel and finely chop the onion. Peel and cut the potatoes, carrots and turnip into 1 cm (½ in) dice, and add to the bowl along with the onion. Mix well, then season with salt and pepper, and add the parsley and a splash each of the sauces.

4 Cut the pastry into four pieces and roll each of them out thinly. Cut into circles of 15 cm (6 in) in diameter. Brush the edges of each pastry circle with egg wash, then pile a quarter of the filling into the middle of each. Spread in a line across the centre of the pastry. Fold the pastry over and up to make a seal on top of the filling. Using your thumb and forefinger, crimp the edges in a wavy fashion. Brush with egg wash and make a hole in the top for the steam to escape.

5 Bake in the preheated oven for 30 minutes, then reduce the oven temperature to 180°C/350°F/Gas 4 and continue to cook for a further 20 minutes. Serve hot or cold.

•You could use rough puff or hot water crust pastry (see page 144) instead of the shortcrust.

Irish Stew

SERVES 4

The combination of lamb, onions and potatoes is common throughout Europe, but the most famous version is that from Ireland, where potatoes were such a staple, and sheep thrived on the lush grazing. Hogget or mutton was probably used at first, and some say that kid was common as well.

The version here is unusual because of the cabbage, but that's how we used to do it at The Savoy Hotel, plating the lamb chops with a separate braised cabbage 'ball', the whole potatoes and the sauce, flavoured and thickened by the potato and cabbage (and sometimes enriched with cream). The celery leaves were the final touch.

900g (2 lb) large potatoes
3 large onions
½ white cabbage
8 large middle neck lamb chops
salt and freshly ground black pepper
600ml (1 pint) white stock (made from
   unroasted bones or vegetables)

1 bouquet garni (bay leaf, parsley, thyme
   etc.)
1 tbsp chopped celery leaves

1 Peel the potatoes and trim into twelve
even-sized pieces. Put to one side in water
and keep the trimmings.

2 Peel and thinly slice the onions, and lay
in the bottom of a large, deep, heatproof
stewing pan. Shred the cabbage and place
on top of the onion. Put the chops on top.
Slice the potato trimmings and scatter over
the chops. Season with salt and pepper.

3 Cover the vegetables and meat with the
stock and add the bouquet garni. Bring up
to the boil, cover with a lid and cook slowly
for 1-1½ hours on top of the stove.

4 Put in the trimmed potatoes, and gently
simmer for another 20-30 minutes until the
potatoes and the chops are cooked. Take out
the chops and whole potatoes, put into a
serving dish and keep warm.

5 Remove the bouquet garni and puree
the liquor in a food processor. Check for
seasoning and consistency.

6 Pour the sauce over the meat, sprinkle
with the chopped celery leaves and serve.

Pot-roasted Shoulder of Lamb

SERVES 6-8

It is said that until the nineteenth century, sheep were valued more for their wool than their meat. Older sheep would have been slaughtered once past their best fleece days, and probably salted for winter eating. Lambs would have been an occasional treat, whereas now of course it is mutton that is rare.

A piece of sheep – or indeed a whole one – would traditionally have been roasted in front of the fire. Here I'm pot-roasting a boned shoulder, a good way of dealing with and dissolving the fat and cartilage of the cut (once very underrated, now becoming popular again, thank goodness). The meat is rolled round garlic (not very British, I admit) and rosemary, and then served with some traditional accompaniments. They say that these 'tracklements' should be made of foods the animals themselves might have eaten, thus the rosemary here, and sheep might very well have eaten wild mint and redcurrants as well.

I have in my mind that if you tie the lamb

correctly, with the remaining bone at the right angle, the lamb looks rather like a duck, which some wag of a parson at some time called Parson's Duck

1 x 2kg (4½ lb) shoulder of lamb
1 bunch fresh rosemary, leaves separated
  from the stalks (keep the latter)
2 garlic cloves, peeled and crushed
salt and freshly ground black pepper
1 tbsp olive oil
2 onions, peeled and roughly chopped
1 celery stalk, roughly chopped
1 large carrot, roughly chopped
25g (1 oz) unsalted butter
150ml (5 fl oz) white wine
300ml (10 fl oz) meat stock

1 Preheat the oven to 180°C/350°F/Gas 4.

2 There are three bones in shoulder of lamb, and we want to take out two of them. If unhappy, get your butcher to do it, but it's really quite easy and because you can't go too far wrong, it's good boning practice for you! Remove the shoulder blade and the 'upper arm' bone from the flesh side by carefully following the bones round. Open up from the centre to create a two-flap pocket.

3 Chop the rosemary leaves, then mix with the crushed garlic and some salt and pepper, and smear into the inner side of the lamb. Roll the lamb up like a Swiss roll, so that it looks like the body of a duck. Tie the shoulder with string to help keep the shape.

4 Heat the oil in a large frying pan, and sear and colour the outside of the lamb until golden brown.

5 Put the vegetables in the bottom of an ovenproof casserole or roasting tray big enough for the lamb. It should have a tight-fitting lid (if not, foil will have to be used). Put the lamb on top of the vegetables and season it. Put in the butter, the white wine and the stalks from the rosemary.

6 Cover with the lid and cook in the preheated moderate oven for 1½ hours. Turn the heat down to 120°C/250°F/Gas ½, and cook for a further hour. The lamb should be well cooked and ready to melt in the mouth (rather like the Greek *kleftiko*).

7 Take the dish out of the oven and allow the lamb to stand for 10 minutes.

8 Meanwhile, pour off the excess fat from the cooking dish, then add the meat stock. Boil together to reduce by about a third, then skim off the fat, strain and serve hot with the meat.

Lancashire Hotpot

SERVES 4

Slow-cooked dishes such as this only evolved properly once people had ovens. As these were few and far between domestically at first, many hotpots were taken to the local baker or cookshop to be cooked (similar dishes in France bear the adjective *'boulangère'* because of this). At home, a hotpot would be cooked in the baking oven as it cooled after the high heat of baking day.

Speaking as a Yorkshireman, I don't know why Lancashire has the kudos of inventing hotpot. However, it's a fantastic dish, traditionally made with neck end chops. I prefer to use chump chops from the other end, as there's less bone, more meat, and they eat well. So could we call this a Yorkshire hotpot?

4 x 225g (8 oz) lamb chump chops on the bone
55g (2 oz) beef dripping
450g (1 lb) large onions, peeled and finely sliced
900g (2 lb) even-sized potatoes

85g (3 oz) unsalted butter, melted
salt and freshly ground black pepper
4 lambs' kidneys, cored and sliced
600ml (1 pint) lamb or chicken stock
1 tbsp chopped fresh chives

1 Preheat the oven to 200°C/400°F/Gas 6.

2 Trim the chops. Heat the dripping in a large frying pan, and colour the chops well on each side. Put to one side. Add the onion to the pan and colour quickly. Pour out into a dish and leave to cool.

3 Peel the potatoes and, if you can be bothered, cut and trim them to a cylindrical shape. (This is what chefs would do, and it looks very impressive.) Then slice into even slices of about 3mm (⅛in) thick.

4 Put a third of the melted butter into the bottom of a large casserole dish. Place a layer of potatoes on top of the butter (keep the best shapes for later) and season. Sprinkle with half the onions, then place the chops on top. Season again. Mix the kidneys with the rest of the onions, then sprinkle over the meat. Pat flat.

5 Carefully arrange the rest of the potatoes overlapping each other to cover the top of the meat and onions. Pour the stock over to come just two-thirds of the way up. Season with salt and pepper, then brush the potato layer carefully with most of the remaining melted butter.

6 Cover the pot with a lid and put into the preheated oven for half an hour. Reduce the oven temperature to 180°C/350°F/Gas 4 and cook for a further 1½ hours.

7 Remove the lid, brush the potatoes again with melted butter and cook on until the potatoes are brown. Remove the casserole from the oven and leave to rest for a few minutes. Sprinkle the potato topping with chopped chives and serve.

•If you like, you could leave out the kidneys and substitute mushrooms as in a steak and kidney pudding or pie.

Mutton Pies

MAKES 4

Large and small pies made with mutton or lamb have been popular since the Middle Ages. At first, like so many meat dishes of the time, they would have been quite sweet, mixed with dried fruit, sugar and sweet spices; later they became more savoury. There are lots of such pies in the north of England (perhaps *the* pie centre of the country) and in Scotland. North of the border they use minced, spiced mutton; in places like Northumberland the meat is chunkier, as here. But both are made with a hot water crust pastry, as is the famous British pork pie.

Apparently mutton pies were admired by Dr Johnson (he also liked Scotch broth), and were served at Balmoral and Buckingham Palace receptions by Queen Victoria and King George V. Fine fare indeed.

25g (1 oz) unsalted butter
1 red onion, peeled and finely chopped
1 tsp chopped fresh rosemary
115g (4 oz) mushrooms, finely chopped
a little vegetable oil
450g (1 lb) shoulder of lamb, off the bone,
    trimmed and cut into 5mm (¼ in) pieces
300ml (10 fl oz) lamb stock
salt and freshly ground black pepper
1 tsp freshly grated nutmeg
1 tsp fécule (potato flour) or cornflour,
    slaked in 1 tbsp lamb stock

Hot water crust pastry
350g (12 oz) plain flour
a pinch of salt

150ml (5 fl oz) water
115g (4 oz) white lard
1 egg yolk
1 egg, mixed with a little water, to glaze

1 Make the filling first. Melt the butter and sweat the finely chopped onion and rosemary without colouring for a few minutes. Add the mushrooms and cook for 3 minutes.

2 Put the meat in a frying pan, and pan-fry in the oil to colour on all sides. Add to the onion mixture along with half the lamb stock and season with salt, pepper and nutmeg. Cover and cook for 30 minutes on top of the stove, then allow to cool.

3 Meanwhile, preheat the oven to 190°C/375°F/Gas 5.

4 To start the pastry, sift the flour and salt into a bowl.

5 Bring the water up to boiling in a medium pan, take off the heat, add the lard and allow it to melt. Add the flour and beat well to amalgamate, then knead until smooth. Stir in the egg yolk and keep warm. Try to work quickly.

6 To use, roll out and cut into rounds to fit

patty tins or muffin moulds of about 10cm (4 in) in diameter. Keep the leftover pastry covered and warm; you need it for the lids.

7 Spoon the cold filling into the pie cases. Roll out the rest of the pastry and cut out the correct lid shapes. Moisten the edges of the pie cases and put the lids on top, pressing to make a seal. Make a hole in the middle, and brush the tops with mixed egg and water to glaze. Bake in the preheated oven for 45 minutes, until the pastry is crisp and golden.

8 Mix the slaked fécule or cornflour with the remaining lamb stock. Bring to the boil gently, stirring, until thickened (this is what chefs call a 'thickened stock').

9 When the pies come out of the oven, re-cut the hole in the top, and carefully pour some thickened stock into each pie. Serve hot or cold.

•Pies such as this are very portable, good for picnics. You could make them in smaller moulds if you liked.

•Note that I haven't asked you to use the pastry in the traditional way, persuading it up around the sides of a jam jar or similar to get the shape. Very hands on and complicated!

Shepherd's Pie

SERVES 4

There are always leftovers from a roast joint, and they can be re-used in a number of ways. Although it's simple, I think shepherd's pie, using lamb, is one of the best – but cottage pie, its beef equivalent, is good too. The recipe is said to have been the creation of shepherds' wives in Cumbria and the Lake District (where the lamb is so good nowadays), who needed to make tough leftover mutton more palatable. Cutting it up small or pounding it would have helped, as would the gravy, but we of course now have the mincer and processor to help us.

Always make plenty of a shepherd's pie, because it's something people always want seconds of. It's more than greed, it's actually psychological!

25g (1 oz) beef dripping or lard
1 large onion, peeled and finely chopped
1 carrot, peeled and diced
450g (1 lb) cooked lamb, minced
1 tsp tomato purée

1-2 garlic cloves, peeled and crushed
  (optional)
15g (½oz) plain flour
300ml (10 fl oz) meat stock
a dash of Worcestershire sauce
1 tbsp chopped fresh parsley
salt and freshly ground black pepper

Potato topping
450g (1 lb) potatoes
2 tbsp double cream
115g (4 oz) unsalted butter
a pinch of freshly grated nutmeg

1 Melt the dripping in a pan and add the onion and carrot (you could have chopped them together in a processor). Cook until soft but not coloured.

2 Add the minced lamb and fry for 2 minutes, then add the tomato purée, garlic if using it, and flour, and mix well. Add the stock and bring to the boil, then simmer for 10-15 minutes until the stew thickens but does not stick to the pan. Stir in the Worcestershire sauce, parsley and some salt and pepper, and remove from the heat. Put into a pie dish of about 850ml (1½ pints) and leave to cool.

3 Peel the potatoes then cut them into even pieces and put into cold salted water.

Bring to the boil and cook until tender, then drain and return to the pan. Put back on the heat to dry out, carefully stirring all the time.

4 Put the double cream and 85g (3 oz) of the butter into a clean pan and bring to the boil. Pass the potatoes through a potato 'ricer' into the cream mixture. Stir well, season with salt and pepper and add some nutmeg. Allow to cool.

5 Preheat the oven to 180°C/350°F/Gas 4.

6 Put the potato into a piping bag with a 2cm (¾in) plain nozzle and pipe on to the meat mixture in the pie dish. Put the pie dish into the preheated oven for 10 minutes: this sets the potato topping.

7 Melt the remaining butter and carefully brush over the top of the pie. Put back in the oven for a further 20 minutes or until golden brown. Serve immediately.

•This is essentially a leftover recipe, but you can make it with fresh lamb (or beef). Buy mince, and cook it with the vegetables for longer than above.

•You don't have to use a piping bag for the potato. Spoon it on evenly, and level with a palette knife dipped in olive oil or melted butter, then scroll to make a pattern.

•When we were very good as kids, my mum used to add some grated cheese to the potatoes and then sprinkle some more on top before baking.

•You can leave out the garlic if you like – a modern addition – or you can add something like fried mushrooms or sun-dried tomatoes.

Roast Loin of Pork with Crackling

SERVES 6-8

Wild pigs – or wild boars as they are more commonly known – once ran free in British forests and were hunted by royalty. But pigs, easy to tame, have been domesticated for thousands of years, and in the Middle Ages, most country people, rich and poor, would have kept at least one pig. This would forage in woodlands, accept scraps and household waste, and generally cause little trouble – and then in the autumn it would provide fresh meat for roasting, and sausages, hams, bacon, black puddings and salted joints for the winter. The pig was probably the most useful animal for, as the saying goes, you could eat everything but the squeak.

Unlike other animals, the pig is sold with its skin on, and it is this which crisps up on roasting, to make crackling. The hoary question is whether to leave the crackling on or not during cooking. If you are marinating the meat, you must obviously take the skin off, but it cooks well on the joint. If you take it off, you can roast it separately between two trays to keep it flat. In Mexico, they sell large strips of crackling that look like prawn crackers, but we of course have our own pork scratchings...

1 x 1.8kg (4 lb) loin of pork
fine salt and 1 tbsp coarse sea salt
1 onion, peeled and sliced
150ml (5 fl oz) dry cider
600ml (1 pint) meat stock
1 small bunch fresh sage

1 Preheat the oven to 220°C/425°F/Gas 7.

2 Wipe the loin with a dry doth. Using a sharp knife, e.g. a Stanley knife, carefully score the rind of the pork from the back to the belly. Score quite deeply through the rind into the fat, but not into the meat. Score 5mm (¼ in) apart and across the length of the joint. Rub the skin with fine salt.

3 Put the meat on a metal trivet in a roasting tray and then into the hot oven for 25 minutes. Turn the oven down to 190°C/375°F/Gas 5 and cook for another 55 minutes approximately. About 10 minutes before the end of cooking, sprinkle the crackling with the sea salt.

4 When cooked take the pork out of the oven, and leave to rest in a warm dry place. Do not pinch all of the crackling!

5 Add the sliced onion to the fat in the tray and fry to colour slightly. Carefully pour off the excess fat (keep to use as dripping for roast potatoes etc.).

6 Add the cider to the onions, and boil to reduce by half, then pour all of this into a saucepan, Add the stock and sage, bring to the boil and reduce until the desired strength of flavour is achieved. Skim off any scum and strain.

7 To serve, take off the crackling by cutting from the back down to the belly. Put this to one side. Take the meat off the bone by cutting down the backbone to the ribs and then over the ribs to release the meat. Cut from the side with a longish knife. Serve slices of the meat with strips of crackling, the hot gravy and some *Apple Sauce* (see page 324).

•Gloucester Old Spot is an old breed with black spots on its skin, said to have been caused by apples falling on them in the orchards where they traditionally foraged. The meat is dense and full of pork flavour.

•Chop off the backbone using a large knife. Keep the ribs, smear them with a honey/soy glaze and reheat to make great spare ribs.

Roast Ham

SERVES 12-16

Means of preserving hams – the cured legs of pig – vary all over the world. In Italy and Spain, they salt-cure and then 'air-dry' the legs to make Parma and serrano hams respectively. In Britain, though, most hams are for cooking: they are soaked in brines of varying flavours, then hung to mature and dry, sometimes smoked, before being boiled and perhaps roasted or baked thereafter.

I'm telling you how to cook a whole piece of gammon here, which is huge, so before embarking on the recipe, make sure you have a pot and oven big enough to hold it. (You can of course use a smaller piece; cut down the proportions and times accordingly.) It's an ideal dish for a party, for family gatherings, or for that Christmas week when cold turkey begins to pall.

1 x 4.5-5.4kg (10-12 lb) gammon
1 onion, peeled and chopped
2 carrots, chopped
2 leeks, chopped
2 apples, chopped (no need to core)
2 bay leaves
a handful of parsley stalks
12 cloves
12 black peppercorns
600ml (1 pint) cider vinegar

Glaze
1 pineapple
175g (6 oz) unrefined demerara sugar
4 tbsp Dijon mustard

1 Soak the ham overnight in cold water to cover (it might be wise to ask your butcher, when buying, how long he thinks you might need to soak).

2 Put the ham into a large pot, and add the chopped vegetables, apples and the herbs and spices. Pour in the vinegar and cover with cold water. Bring slowly up to the boil and then turn down to simmer. Skim off the scum. Put on a lid, propping it slightly open with a wooden spoon to prevent boiling over, and allow to simmer gently for approximately 3-4 hours.

3 To test if done, either stick a large roasting fork in (if cooked it will come out easily), or if using a whole gammon (much preferred), a small bone that sticks out at the knuckle end will be easy to release when wiggled.

4 When cooked, leave the ham in the stock for 20 minutes to rest. If serving hot and boiled, drain well and serve.

5 But if roasting, drain, then remove the skin first of all. This will easily pull off from the body end, not the knuckle end. Then trim off the excess fat using a sharp knife, trying all the time to retain the shape of the leg.

6 Preheat the oven to 200°C/400°F/Gas 6.

7 To make the glaze, peel the pineapple and put the chopped flesh through the processor. Drain the flesh well, keeping the juice for the sauce. Mix the pineapple pulp with the sugar.

8 Brush the mustard over the fat of the ham, then carefully press the pineapple mixture over the ham. Score the sugar carefully in parallel lines one way and then at an angle to make diamonds of white lines.

9 Put into the preheated oven for about 20 minutes until the sugar caramelises. Take the ham out, leave to stand for 10 minutes, and then carve.

•Check the stock. If it's not too salty, keep it for soups (great in the pea soup on page 15), or a parsley sauce which would be perfect with the ham, whether boiled or roasted (see page 153). Otherwise the *Cumberland Sauce* on page 328 would be good with it when served cold, as would the *Piccalilli* (see page 310).

•You will have plenty of ham left over for sandwiches, cold meats, or for putting into mixtures.

Calf's Liver with Sage, Caper and Sherry Sauce

SERVES 4

We once ate very much more offal than we do now. Liver, as one of the more reasonable *looking* of the various 'off-falls', has always been popular, and has usually been fried with onions or with bacon. It can be stewed too, and one such dish made with ox liver, sage and a sliced potato topping is known as Yorkshireman's Goose...

For this dish I've used calf's liver, but you could substitute lamb's livers if you can find them. I've also used sage, as the Yorkshiremen did above, but have added some capers and sherry for extra flavour. Neither is native to Britain, but both have been appreciated for many centuries, sherry especially. It was Sir Francis Drake who introduced Jerez 'sack' to England when he appropriated several thousand barrels from Cadiz while 'singeing the King of Spain's beard'. The name 'Jerez' was gradually anglicised to 'sherry' (the 'sack' was dropped), and in the succeeding centuries, the popularity of the drink grew. Adventurers from all over Britain went to Jerez to make their fortunes, and many of the names of the great sherry houses – Harvey's, Croft's etc. – reflect this still.

4 x 1 cm (½ in) thick slices calf's liver, about 140-175g (5-6 oz) total weight
2 tbsp olive oil
salt and freshly ground black pepper
55g (2 oz) butter
2 shallots, peeled and finely chopped
2 tbsp midget capers (they're tiny and expensive!)
150ml (5 fl oz) dry sherry
1 splash sherry vinegar (or lemon juice)
1 tbsp chopped fresh sage
150ml (5 fl oz) veal stock
1 tsp fécule (potato flour) or cornflour, slaked in 1 tbsp water

1 Trim the liver well, cutting out any large tubes. The butcher should have removed the filmy skin.

2 Heat the olive oil in a frying pan until very hot. Lay the liver slices in carefully, but do not over-fill the pan. Cook in two batches if necessary. When golden brown, turn over, cook quickly and take out. Put to one side, season and keep warm.

3 Throw away excess oil from the pan and

melt half of the butter in it. Add the shallots and capers, and sauté to soften, but do not colour. Add the dry sherry and reduce by half. Add the sherry vinegar, sage, stock and the slaked fécule or cornflour. Bring up to the boil, stirring until it thickens, then add the remaining butter. Shake in until melted.

4 Reheat the liver quickly, serve on warm plates and pour the sauce over.

•I think the thickness of liver to be fried is very important, with each slice no thicker than specified overleaf, but it's up to you.

•Good served with buttery mashed potato or *pommes lyonnaise*, sautéed potatoes and onions.

Mustard-devilled Calf's Kidneys

SERVES 4

Lamb's kidneys, still encased in their own suet, were once grilled whole and served, split open, on toast – a favourite breakfast for Edwardian gentlemen. Those same worthies also liked them at the other end of the day, devilled on toast, as a savoury after dinner. I'm using calf's kidney here, but lamb's kidneys can be substituted.

You either love kidneys or hate them, and I'm of the former persuasion. I associate them with José, who opened up at Turner's for fourteen years, and put our stockpots on (he's now retired to Spain). When veal, pork or lamb loins came in, José would take the kidneys off, divest them of their fat, and grill them with garlic. Served on good toast, they were my best start to the day ever.

2 whole calf's kidneys in their fat
a splash of olive oil
25g (1 oz) butter
2 shallots, peeled and finely chopped
150ml (5 fl oz) dry white wine
150ml (5 fl oz) double cream
3 tbsp grain mustard
1 tbsp chopped fresh chervil
salt and freshly ground black pepper
Tabasco sauce

1 Preheat the oven to 220°C/425°F/Gas 7.

2 Trim the excess fat from the kidneys using a knife, but try to retain the original shape. Sear and colour the kidneys on all sides in a little oil in a hot frying pan. Put into the preheated hot oven, and roast for 15 minutes. Take out and leave to rest.

3 Meanwhile, melt the butter and sauté the shallots, but do not let them colour. Add the wine and boil to reduce by two-thirds. Add the cream and bring to the boil. Boil to reduce by a third. Take off the heat and stir in the mustard and chervil. Check for seasoning and consistency.

4 Thinly slice the kidneys and arrange on a hot plate to fill the plate. Collect all the juices from the kidneys and pour into the sauce. Add Tabasco to taste (careful, it's hot), then warm the sauce through again.

5 Spoon the sauce over the kidneys and serve immediately.

5

Poultry and Game

At one time, all the meat eaten by the British was 'game' – elk, deer, wild ox, wild pig and birds of every description. As we domesticated cattle, pigs and sheep, so we did the same with birds such as geese, ducks and chickens. The Romans were probably a major influence, for they introduced and intensively reared birds such as peacocks, pheasants and guinea fowl (as well as rabbits, dormice and snails).

For centuries, because of the difficulty of keeping the 'great meat' animals (cattle, sheep and pigs) over the winter, poultry birds and game birds and animals would have provided a major source of fresh meat. Nothing was omitted, and many birds we wouldn't dream of eating now were enjoyed: swan, bustard, stork, blackbirds, finches, larks... (I once met a Paris chef who specialised in game of this nature when I was at The Capital. The chef himself was in his eighties, and his kitchen 'boys' must have been in their sixties. They wore aprons that looked as if they hadn't been taken off

163

since the day they started!) Rabbit and hare were eaten by rich and poor alike – when game laws did not bar the latter from hunting – but venison was always for the aristocracy alone.

Almost every household, however poor, would have had a few hens but they were too valuable as egg-layers to eat. Only when old, scrawny and beyond egg-laying might they be consigned to the poor man's cooking pot (and, as we know, the stock from an older chicken is much more flavourful). The rich, however, would have relished poultry much more often: roasting chickens, geese, ducks and pigeons on the spit, cooking them in pottages and pies, and potting them in butter.

Because poultry and game were so readily available on the whole, they were less well thought of in culinary terms than red meat (as was fish). However, curiously, a roasted bird was often considered a food for celebrations – the goose at harvest festival, and originally at Christmas, before the interloper turkey became the norm. I remember chicken – often tasting of the fishmeal in its diet – being a very special treat for Sunday lunch. Nowadays chicken is so common that we are tending to ignore it again. Rabbit too, once the most available of wild meats (and therefore the least appreciated), is making a comeback in popularity.

Seasonality is one of the joys of British food and game is perhaps the prime example.

Roast Chicken with Bread Sauce

SERVES 4

As with all other meats, 'roast' chicken would once have been cooked on a spit in front of a fire, instead of in an oven. A young cockerel would normally have been used, as hens were far too valuable as egg-layers. Nowadays, we can get chickens aplenty, but when cooking them as simply as this, do try and buy the very best you can, preferably corn-fed and free-range.

Bread sauce is perhaps the oldest British sauce, dating from medieval times. The Scots claim it as a northern invention, but it appears all over the islands, and is good with most roast birds, domesticated or wild.

1 x 1.6kg (3¼ lb) free-range roasting
    chicken, cleaned weight
salt and freshly ground black pepper
25g (1 oz) lard
55g (2 oz) unsalted butter

Bread sauce

300ml (10 fl oz) milk
150ml (5 f l oz) double cream
1 onion, peeled and stuck with 6 cloves
1 bay leaf
approx. 75g (2¾ oz) fresh white breadcrumbs
25g (1 oz) unsalted butter

1 Preheat the oven to 200°C/400°F/Gas 6.

2 Take out the wishbone, and truss the chicken back to its original shape. Lay it on its side and crush the backbone to allow the chicken to sit on its side and not to spring back to shape. Season the chicken.

3 Heat the lard in a heatproof and ovenproof dish, then add the butter and the chicken lying on one side to start to colour. If the breast touches the fat as well, put a little piece of potato under it to protect it.

4 Roast in the preheated oven for 20 minutes, then turn the chicken on to its other side and cook in the same way, making sure that the legs in both instances are touching the fat, for 20 more minutes.

5 Turn the bird over on to its back and baste with lard and butter. Turn the oven down to 180°C/350°F/Gas 4 and roast until ready. To test after 10 minutes, pierce the thickest part of the thigh: if the juices run clear, the bird is cooked. If not, roast for a little longer.

6 Leave to rest for 10 minutes in a warm place before carving.

7 Meanwhile, make the bread sauce. Bring the milk and cream up to the boil with the onion, cloves and bay leaf. Leave to sit for 10 minutes then add the breadcrumbs. Stir until smooth, then take out the onion. Add the butter and some salt and pepper. Cover with clingfilm or buttered paper.

8 To carve the chicken, first take off the strings. Turn it on to its side and cut the skin between the leg and the breast. Now pull the leg away using a carving knife, pulling away from the neck. This will release the meat. (It will also expose the little hidden nugget of meat, the cook's treat, the oyster. Eat it and don't tell anyone.) Put the leg on a chopping board and chop to separate the thigh from the drumstick. Turn the bird over and repeat.

9 Stand the bird on its back and carve down one side of the breastbone, bringing the knife down between the wing and neck joints. Do the same on the other side. Cut each breast in two.

10 Serve the thigh with the smaller piece of breast, and the drumstick with the other. Offer the bread sauce and gravy if you like (see below) separately. (And some roast potatoes, cooked chipolatas and bacon rolls would make for the full monty!)

•Stages 3–4 may seem complicated, but this is the best way to cook any fleshy bird. As legs are always tougher than breasts, they take longer to cook. By placing the legs directly on the heated dish, in the hot fat – and protecting the breast from that same exposure – both should be cooked at about the same time.

•To make a gravy with the pan juices, thinly slice half an onion and throw into the roasting pan. Fry quickly so that the onion absorbs the juices, then carefully pour away the excess fat (this can be used again). I now like to add a drop of wine, but this isn't classically British. Add some chicken stock, bring to the boil and reduce. Strain into a clean pan, skim off any excess fat, and check for seasoning. Many British gravies have some flour in them to form a sauce-like gravy, but my take on gravy, particularly with chicken, is that it should be thin.

Poached Chicken with Parsley Sauce

SERVES 4

Poaching or boiling would once have been the commonest method of cooking chicken (usually a tough old hen past her best laying days), and there was the added bonus of a delicious stock with which to make a soup. Here I've used the stock to make a wonderful sauce, full of the flavour of the chicken, and thickened with lots of butter and parsley. The sauce is an echo of the traditional green herb sauce of medieval times, in which parsley played a major part.

1 x 1.6kg (3½ lb) free-range chicken,
  cleaned weight
1 lemon, halved
2 onions, peeled and chopped
1 leek, cleaned and chopped
2 celery stalks, chopped
1 bay leaf
6 cloves
salt and freshly ground black pepper

Parsley sauce
600ml (1 pint) reduced chicken stock (see
  method)
300ml (10 fl oz) double cream
115g (4 oz) cold unsalted butter, diced
3 tbsp chopped fresh parsley

1 Remove the wishbone from the chicken.
Trim and tie the chicken to its proper shape.
Rub the outside of the chicken with the
fresh lemon to keep the skin white.

2 Put the chicken into a large pot and add
the chopped onion, leek and celery, the bay
leaf, cloves and a little salt and pepper.
Cover with water and bring up to the boil.
Pull to one side, and clean off any scum that
arises.

3 Cover with a lid for the first half-hour
simmering slowly, then bring to the boil.
Remove the lid, and slowly cook for a
further hour, skimming occasionally. To
check if the bird is cooked, push a skewer
into the thickest part of the thigh: if the
juices run clear or a little pinkish, then the
bird is cooked. If the juices are at all red,
then the bird needs a bit longer.

4 When the chicken is cooked, remove
from the stock and keep in a warm place.
Use a clean tea towel, dipped in the stock

and squeezed out, to cover the bird and keep it from drying out.

5 Strain the stock into a clean pan (or two) and boil to reduce by about half – or until the stock has a good, round, concentrated flavour.

6 Put 600ml (1 pint) of this stock into a separate pan, and the cream into the original stock pan. Reduce the cream until it thickens, and then add the stock. Reduce again until you have a sauce-like consistency.

7 Check for seasoning, then add the butter and swirl the pan to melt the butter dice. Add the chopped parsley.

8 Carve the bird into two drumsticks, two thighs, two wing pieces and then the breast in half. Arrange the pieces in a dish and pour the sauce over and around.

•At stage 5, using two pans means that the stock reduces more quickly, so the chicken doesn't hang around too long.

•At stage 7, the professional chef in me would always strain the sauce through a fine sieve to make it absolutely smooth before adding the parsley. However, if you can't be bothered, I can understand...

Roast Goose Stuffed with Apple and Fig

SERVES 6

Goose was the celebratory bird in Olde England before the turkey was known, and it still serves that role in much of Europe. Although geese were valued, they had rather a hard time of it. If caught eating someone's corn in Wales, they could be executed (a good excuse to eat goose?). They were force-fattened in much the same way as *foie gras* ducks and geese are in France today. They were plucked regularly throughout the year to supply quills and down (which rendered them rather tough), and then they could be marched off to London (with tarred feet like turkeys) to feed the capital's multitudes.

Geese are traditionally best in September, when they were fattened on stubble and eaten on Michaelmas Day, the 29th.

1 x 7.25kg (16 lb) goose
salt and freshly ground black pepper

Stuffing
10 slices dried bread, broken into pieces

2 Cox's apples, grated
4 ripe figs, pulped with a fork
1 onion, peeled and finely chopped
1 tbsp chopped fresh sage
1 small egg
2 tbsp cider
2 tbsp Calvados
unsalted butter

Glaze
2 tbsp runny honey
1 tbsp Calvados
juice of ½ lemon

1 Preheat the oven to 220°C/425°F/Gas 7.

2 To prepare the goose, take out the wishbone and then remove the excess fat from the cavity end.

3 For the stuffing, mix all the ingredients together except for the butter, and season well with salt and pepper.

4 Use a quarter of this stuffing to stuff the neck end of the goose, and put the rest separately in an ovenproof dish greased with butter.

5 Before roasting the goose, prick all over the breast and neck end to allow the excess fat to be released. Put the bird in a roasting tray on a rack and roast in the preheated oven for 30 minutes. Turn the oven down to 180°C/350°F/Gas 4 and cook for a further 2 hours.

6 Take the bird out and pour the fat from the tray (keep to use for cooking roast potatoes etc.). Put the goose back into the same temperature oven, along with the dish of stuffing, which needs to roast for an hour. Cook the goose for a further 30 minutes on its breast, not on the rack, then turn it on to its back.

7 Mix together the honey, Calvados and lemon juice for the glaze, and brush over the breast of the bird. Cook for a final 30 minutes, basting regularly with the glaze.

8 Remove the goose from the oven, and leave to rest for 20 minutes before carving.

•A tart sauce or stuffing is normal with goose: apple in the autumn (the fig here is an interesting but not untraditional addition) and, in spring, sorrel would be good.

Braised Duck with Peas

SERVES 4

Ducks from Aylesbury were becoming popular in the London markets of the eighteenth century, and in many cookery books thereafter (although some say it's a Roman or Elizabethan idea) they were boiled with turnips. I remember at The Savoy we used to cook our duck with turnips too, along with olives and cream. However, peas are traditional with ducklings as well – possibly because they are in season at about the same time of year – and that too became a popular braising combination. Lettuce was often added, which is a French touch, and indeed some old cookbooks describe the dish as '*à la française*', in the French fashion.

Some recipes add cream to the peas and then puree them for a sauce, but I don't think this is necessary. The simple step of braising them and the lettuce in with the duck gives amazing flavour.

2 x 1.1kg (2½ lb) ducks, with giblets
600ml (1 pint) duck or chicken stock
85g (3 oz) butter

225g (8 oz) bacon in the piece, cut into
  stubby strips (lardons) of about 5 x 5mm
  x 2.5cm (¼ x ¼ x 1 in)
salt and freshly ground black pepper
175g (6 oz) small button onions (12 plus),
  peeled
1 round lettuce, shredded at the last
  minute
450g (1 lb) frozen peas
1 tbsp each of chopped fresh sage, mint
  and parsley

1 Take the giblets out of the ducks. Put the giblets into the stock and leave to gently simmer for 30 minutes.

2 Preheat the oven to 160°C/325°F/Gas 3.

3 Melt 25g (1 oz) of the butter in a casserole dish large enough to hold both ducks. Add the bacon lardons and button onions, and gently colour on all sides. When nicely coloured, take out and keep on one side.

4 Prick the ducks all over with a fork, and rub with a little salt. Colour all over in the same dish as the lardons and onions, then take out of the dish. Drain off all the fat and put the ducks back in the dish.

5 Strain the stock into the dish along with

the ducks, bring to the boil and cover with the lid. Put into the preheated oven and cook for 1½ hours.

6 Add the button onions and lardons, and braise for a further 15 minutes.

7 Take the ducks out and allow to rest, keeping them warm.

8 Remove excess fat from the juices in the dish, then add the shredded lettuce, peas and herbs. Simmer to reduce this sauce by a third. Correct the seasoning and consistency, then swirl in the remaining butter.

9 Carve the ducks and put on a flat dish. Pour the sauce over and serve immediately.

Roast Grouse

SERVES 4

The red grouse is said to be the king of game birds, and although the flesh is delicious, its popularity has probably got more to do with its rarity – you almost need the wealth of a king in order to shoot it, buy it or eat it. The Glorious Twelfth, the twelfth of August, is when the season starts, and London restaurateurs still compete to have the first birds flown down from Scotland – the birds' only habitat – to be on their tables that very night. The season is short, only until the tenth of December (although the grouse would probably think it too long). Grouse are not raised for the shoot, as are other game birds like pheasant, but the heather moors where they live are very carefully managed to provide the right conditions, cover, nesting places and food. It is probably their diet that makes their flesh more aromatic – they eat heather shoots, flowers and seeds, as well as any wild blaeberries that come their way.

4 young grouse, with giblets
salt and freshly ground black pepper
4 thin slices pork back fat
85g (3 oz) unsalted butter
1 tbsp vegetable oil
4 slices bread
1 onion, peeled and sliced
300ml (10 fl oz) game stock
4 small bunches watercress

1 Preheat the oven to 200°C/400°F/Gas 6.

2 Season well inside the birds, and keep the livers to one side. Tie the pieces of back fat over the breasts of the birds.

3 Heat 25g (1 oz) of the butter and the oil together in a roasting tray, and colour the birds all over.

4 Put the birds in the preheated oven for 15 minutes, then turn the temperature down to 180°C/350°F/Gas 4 and cook for a further 10 minutes. Take the string and back fat off and colour the birds for a final 10 minutes. Keep medium-rare to medium. There's an art to cooking grouse. It should be pink but not bloody. Take out of the oven and leave to rest.

5 Meanwhile toast the bread, then cut 5cm (2 in) circles from each slice.

6 Stew the livers in half the remaining butter, then put into a bowl with the rest of the butter, season well and mash together.

7 Put the onion into the fat in the grouse roasting tray and fry quickly to colour. Add the stock and bring to the boil, season and strain.

8 Put the mushed-up livers on the circles of toast and perch a bird on top of each. Put a bunch of watercress into each cavity, and serve immediately. Serve the gravy separately.

•You can tell young grouse by their undeveloped spurs, and downy breast feathers. Hang them in the feather by the neck for two to three days, no longer.

•Try to get sheets of pork fat. They will cover and moisten the breasts better – vital with the lean flesh of game birds – and they will not flavour it like bacon.

•Serve with game chips, a green vegetable, fried breadcrumbs, bread sauce (see page 166) and redcurrant jelly (the *Apple and Rowan Jelly* on page 318 would be good too). Grouse are also delicious when cold.

Braised Pigeons

SERVES 4

It was the Romans in Britain who encouraged wild pigeons to nest in special *columbaria*, tall towers with hundreds of individual nesting boxes. In the many centuries since then, pigeons were one of the few forms of fresh meat available, and the Roman idea was continued, with dovecotes built into the sides of or on top of monasteries and houses. Wild wood pigeons are shot in the countryside – as much a crop pest now as then but are only available in specialist butchers or poulterers. Squabs, or young pigeons, are now bred for the table, particularly in France.

This recipe is a slightly sophisticated version of more traditional recipes. Once pigeons would have been braised for very much longer because they were older and tougher (for almost as soon as a pigeon takes to flight, its muscles toughen).

6 young pigeons
2 tbsp olive oil
6 shallots, peeled and sliced
1 tsp freshly grated nutmeg
1 small bunch fresh parsley
1 garlic clove, peeled and crushed
1 bay leaf
4 tomatoes
150ml (5 fl oz) Madeira
salt and freshly ground black pepper
150ml (5 fl oz) chicken stock
115g (4 oz) unsalted butter
225g (8 oz) button mushrooms, sliced

1 Preheat the oven to 200°C/400°F/Gas 6.

2 Sprinkle the pigeons with half the oil and roast in the preheated oven for 10 minutes. Remove from the oven, and cut the

legs and backbone away from the breasts, leaving what is called the crown of the pigeons.

3 Put the shallots and remaining oil into a casserole and place the pigeon breasts on top. Put the legs into the casserole as well, and add the nutmeg, parsley, garlic, bay leaf tomatoes (which you have squeezed in your hands first) and Madeira. Season well and add the chicken stock. Bring to the boil, put the lid on and put into the same temperature oven for 15 minutes.

4 Take out of the oven. Remove the breasts and keep them warm while you reduce the sauce by half on the stove top.

5 Melt 25g (1 oz) of the butter in a clean pan and cook the mushrooms until golden brown.

6 Strain the stock, pushing down to extract the last drops of flavour from the vegetables, herbs and pigeon legs. Add the stock to the mushrooms along with the rest of the butter. Shake this into the sauce so that it starts to thicken.

7 Carve the breasts from the bones and put into a serving dish. Add any blood or juices to the sauce. Check the seasoning and pour over the breasts, three per person.

•Pigeons can be shot all year round, but are best between August and October (when fat from all the summer crop-stealing). Young birds have pink legs: the legs darken as the birds age. Or buy from a reliable butcher or game dealer.

•Pigeon legs are very difficult to cook and eat as they are so small, so this is a good way of using them, to get flavour into the sauce.

•This would be an ideal way of cooking pigeon for a game pie. Just put some pastry on the top and put into the oven to get crisp, brown and hot.

Game Pie

SERVES 4

Game was once the most plentiful fresh meat available in Britain, until royal laws were passed and it became an offence for the ordinary man to snare a rabbit or game bird for the family pot. Because the birds obtained (whether legally or by poaching) were often older, they would be encased in suet and steamed for hours as a pudding, or braised first and then covered with a pastry crust as a pie.

Pigeon pie is a speciality of Yorkshire, where young pigeons are cooked with chunks of steak, bacon and hard-boiled eggs under pastry. I've added partridges here as well – in fact you could substitute virtually anything, pheasant or rabbit for instance – and the quails' eggs are a nice modern Turner touch.

225g (8 oz) puff pastry
1 egg yolk, mixed with a little water, to
  glaze

Filling
55g (2 oz) butter
4 smoked bacon rashers, chopped into
  5mm (¼ in) wide strips
2 shallots, peeled and chopped
4 pigeon breasts
4 partridge breasts
salt and freshly ground black pepper
2 tbsp chopped fresh parsley
8 quails' eggs, hard-boiled and shelled
1 tsp Worcestershire sauce
150ml (5 fl oz) chicken stock

1 Melt half the butter in a frying pan and cook the bacon for 2 minutes to colour. Add the finely chopped shallot, cook for a few minutes to soften, then remove both from the pan using a slotted spoon. Put to one side.

2 Melt the remaining butter in the same pan to mix with the bacon fat. Remove the skin from the pigeon and partridge breasts, then seal and colour the flesh in the hot fat. Season and leave to cool.

3 Put a third of the bacon mixture in the bottom of a 1.2 litre (2 pint) pie dish. Lay the pigeon breasts on top and season again. Sprinkle with half of the remaining bacon mixture and half the parsley. Lay the quails' eggs on top along with the partridge breasts, then season. Sprinkle with the remaining bacon mixture and parsley.

4 Mix the Worcestershire sauce with the stock, and pour gently over the ingredients in the pie dish.

5 Preheat the oven to 220°C/425°F/Gas 7.

6 Roll out the puff pastry and cut to make a strip that will fit around the edges of the pie dish, and a large piece to fit the top. Dampen the edges of the dish and lay a thin strip of puff pastry around. Seal to the dish. Dampen the edges of the pastry shape and arrange on top of the strip around the pie

dish edges. Crimp the edges to seal. Brush all over the pastry with egg wash, and decorate with a fork. Cut a hole in the centre for the steam to escape.

7 Bake in the preheated oven for 20 minutes, and then reduce the temperature to 180°C/350°F/Gas 4. Cook for a further 40 minutes or so, covering the pastry with foil if getting too brown. Serve hot.

•Breasts of game birds are now available from supermarkets, but if you buy or acquire the birds whole, cut the breasts off to use in the pie, and use the skins and carcasses to make a wonderful game stock.

Venison Stew

SERVES 4

For centuries, the peasants had to stand back when wild deer raided their kitchen gardens, for they were not allowed to kill them. Deer and venison have always been the prerogative of the aristocracy, and the only taste others might have had would be of 'umbles' (offal) pie. Poachers were hung, drawn, quartered, executed and, later, transported. Luckily venison is now farmed, and we can enjoy its gamey flavour without looking over our shoulders...

This is a classic meat stew recipe. You could do exactly the same with beef, lamb or pork, altering the vegetables, and the jelly flavouring.

675g (1½ lb) venison (shoulder or
    haunch)
2 tbsp olive oil
2 garlic cloves, peeled and crushed
450g (1 lb) tomatoes
2 large carrots, trimmed and finely diced
300ml (10 fl oz) red wine
1 bunch mixed herbs (parsley, sage,
    thyme), tied together
salt and freshly ground black pepper
a little brown stock (made from roasted
    bones), to moisten if needed
2 tbsp redcurrant jelly
12 small cooked new potatoes
12 pre-cooked chestnuts

1 Preheat the oven to 160°C/325°F/Gas 3.

2 Cut the venison into large dice of 2.5cm (1 in) square.

3 Heat the oil in a casserole dish and colour the meat on all sides, Add the garlic, tomatoes and carrots, and cook for 5 min-

utes. Add the wine, herbs and seasoning, cover with a lid and cook in the preheated oven for up to 2 hours, until the meat is tender. Add a little stock if needed.

4 Lift the meat out of the dish and put to one side. Discard the herbs.

5 Add the redcurrant jelly to the juices and vegetables, then liquidise.

6 Put this sauce back on the stove, add the cooked new potatoes and chestnuts, and bring back to the boil. Add the meat and reheat gently.

7 Serve with mashed potato. Some *Apple and Rowan Jelly* (see page 318) would be a good accompaniment.

Rabbit with Mustard

SERVES 6

Like pigeons, rabbits were bred – in special *leporaria* – by the Romans when they came to Britain. Rabbits are actually native to Iberia, and after being introduced to various other parts of the Roman Empire, became a pest as well as a good source of fresh meat. The people of the Balearic Islands had to call for help from the Emperor when they were overrun – and remember what happened more recently in Australia. If we're not careful, according to present-day farmers, and despite myxomatosis, there's a great danger that rabbits will once again become a pest.

Rabbit would once have been the most common game animal, available to rich and poor alike. Although it is not now so popular (probably because of the pet connection, I wasn't allowed to use rabbit on *This Morning* in case children were watching), there are still a good number of recipes in the British tradition. Most of these, as in France and elsewhere in Europe, flavour the generally mild meat with strong spices such as the mustard here, which adds moisture at the same time.

2 small wild rabbits, skinned
600ml (1 pint) chicken stock
150ml (5 fl oz) white wine
3 tbsp Dijon mustard
salt and freshly ground black pepper
1 tbsp olive oil
1 carrot
1 onion
2 celery stalks
½ tsp freshly grated nutmeg

150ml (5 fl oz) double cream
1 tbsp grain mustard
2 tbsp lemon juice
2 tbsp chopped fresh parsley

1 Preheat the oven to 200°C/400°F/Gas 6.

2 Cut the rabbits into pieces: four back legs and four shoulders (the front legs). Trim the saddles, removing the belly, and cut each saddle in half to give four pieces in all.

3 Chop the rest of the carcass and put into a pan with the belly pieces, the chicken stock and white wine. Boil to reduce this stock by half.

4 Meanwhile, mix the Dijon mustard with some salt and pepper and the olive oil. Smear this over the rabbit pieces.

5 Prepare the vegetables and chop into fine dice. Put these in the bottom of a casserole, then lay the rabbit pieces on top. Sprinkle the grated nutmeg over, cover and cook in the preheated oven for 20 minutes.

6 Turn the rabbit pieces over and strain the stock into the casserole. Put back into the oven for a further 20 minutes or until cooked. Take out the pieces of rabbit, place in a clean pan and keep warm.

7 Add the cream to the stock left in the casserole and bring up to the boil. Strain into the clean pan with the rabbit, add the grain mustard and lemon juice, and bring back to the boil.

8 Check the seasoning, add the parsley and serve.

•I had the most fantastic rabbit dish recently in Menorca. The rabbit pieces – legs and saddle – were marinated in oil and garlic, and then barbecued.

•Wild rabbits have much more flavour, but less meat, than hutch-bred rabbits. And remember that rabbits have lots of small bones, so do be careful.

Chunky Tomato Soup

Glamorgan Sausages

Fish Pie

Salad of Scallops with Bacon

Prawn Cocktail

Cornish Pasties

Scotch Woodcock

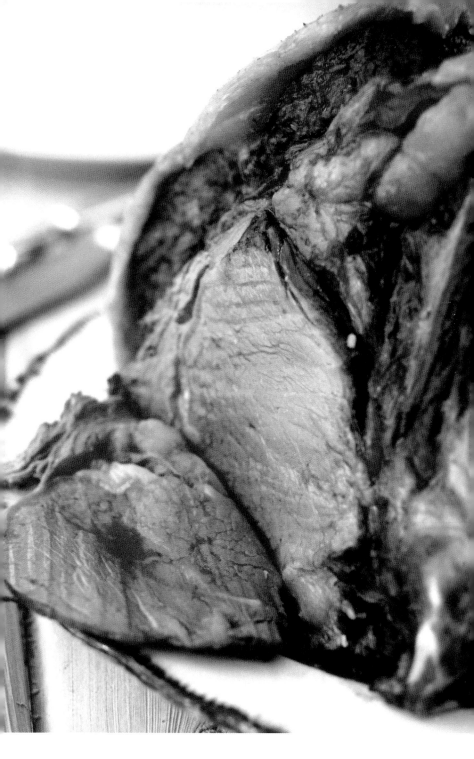

Roast Beef

Shepherd's Pie

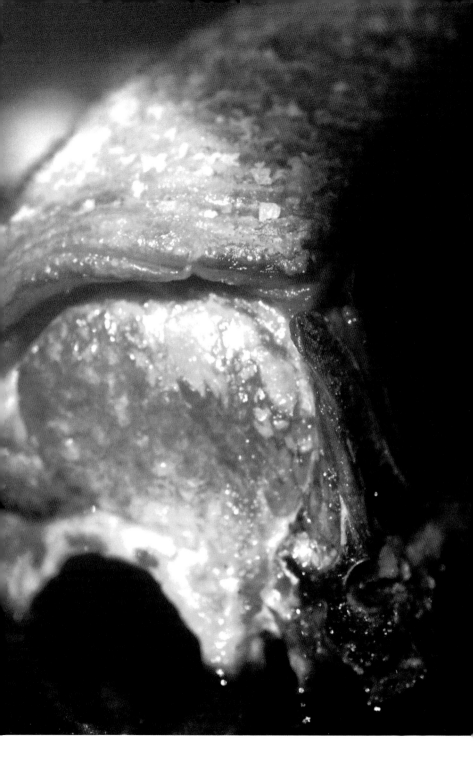

Roast Loin of Pork with Crackling

Calf's Liver with Sage, Caper and Sherry Sauce

Game Pie

Broad Bean and Bacon Salad

Bubble and Squeak

Apple Charlotte

Rice Pudding

Queen of Puddings

Geonese Sponge

Scotch Pancakes

Chelsea Buns

Parkin

Mince Pies

Sage and Onion Stuffing

Horseradish Sauce

6

Vegetables

Vegetables were once a major part of the diet of the poor, who could not afford to eat meat. The native root vegetables such as turnips, parsnips and carrots would be boiled in pottage (probably *over*boiled), with onions and perhaps alongside some grain (or meat if they were lucky). Broad beans and peas would be dried rather than eaten fresh, and it is 'peasant' pulse and protein combinations that have survived, such as beans and bacon and pork and pease pudding. Vegetable cooking was actually rather boring.

After the great transatlantic explorations of the sixteenth century, unknown vegetables were introduced to Europe, among them potatoes, tomatoes, maize (sweetcorn), green beans, peppers and pumpkin. None was accepted very enthusiastically at first, either here or on the Continent, although Ireland, too wet for successful grain cultivation, was quick to adopt the potato, by about 1650. (This disastrous reliance on one crop alone led to the starvation and mass emigration of the populace in the 1840s after potato blight struck.) Gardeners in France, Italy and the Low Countries were also developing new types of vegetable, and as these were introduced to Britain, so vegetables – among them celery, broccoli, Brussels sprouts and artichokes – started to become more popular and more fashionable (at least with the recipe-writing and recipe-reading classes).

It was only at this time that vegetables were defined as a separate category of food, plants grown especially to be eaten. We are fond of vegetables now, and grow them for pleasure, not for necessity. We also cook and treat vegetables properly. Chefs like Paul Gaylor have actually made a speciality of cooking vegetables in an exciting way, and we now have farmers' markets, to which growers bring their produce, often organic, always very fresh.

We are enjoined to eat lots of vegetables for health, and the 'five a day' campaign – eating five portions of fruit and vegetables every day – is a very easy target, especially for children. If we can get children to eat healthy foods as early as possible, and to enjoy them, we will, hopefully, have prevented the tide of obesity that has been worrying us so much lately.

Asparagus

SERVE ABOUT 6 THICK STEMS PER PORTION

The Romans were apparently very fond of asparagus, and perhaps, like so many other foodstuffs, they were responsible for its introduction to Britain. It has always been a vegetable for the rich rather than the poor, as an asparagus bed takes up so much garden space – and only produces a result for less than two months per year.

Asparagus is imported from many countries throughout the world, but I have to say I really do prefer the English spears that arrive in late May, early June – thin (sprue) or fatter, and always green.

1 Using a potato peeler or the back of a strong knife, scrape the lower two-thirds of the stem. Always peel from the tip end to the base and try to get uniformity in look. Much of the flavour and goodness is in the skin, so you only want to remove the outer tough layer. Lay the stems side by side with the tips all levelled up, and cut the lower parts of the stems off so that each stem is

the same length. Tie carefully into bundles.

2 One way to cook the asparagus is to stand them upright in an asparagus basket in boiling water up to three-quarters of the height of the asparagus stems with the top section, the tips, steaming. When cooked the stems will just have a little 'give' about 5cm (2 in) down from the top of the tip or, when the tip of a knife is inserted, they feel only just tender. (It is not essential to stand asparagus stems upright to cook, however. You can plunge the untied spears into boiling salted water in a large wide pan.)

3 When they are cooked, plunge into iced water to stop the cooking and then reheat in boiling water before draining and serving.

4 To serve, put the stems on to a plate, with an upturned fork under the stem end side. This means that they are not covered with sauce and can be picked up without dirtying the hands.

5 Serve with a hollandaise sauce (see page 76), or a melted butter sauce (add 225g/8 oz pieces of cold butter to 1 tbsp cold water and the juice of ½ lemon; whisk over heat to make an emulsion).

Potato Salad

SERVES 4

I don't expect this is very traditionally British – is it an American import? – but it has become part of our repertoire and, sadly, is often very badly done. But a good potato salad is a joy, perfect on a buffet or at a barbecue, and deserves much more respect. I give you a couple of ideas below. Both are great with ham, beef or any cold meat.

Version One

450g (1 lb) waxy potatoes, washed
1 onion, peeled and finely chopped
150ml (5 fl oz) mayonnaise
salt and freshly ground black pepper
chopped fresh chives

1 Cook the potatoes in boiling water in their skins. When tender, drain them and leave to cool.

2 Skin the potatoes and cut them into 5mm (¼ in) dice. Mix with the onion, mayonnaise and salt and pepper to taste. Add the chopped chives.

Version Two

450g (1 lb) new potatoes, washed
150ml (5 fl oz) chicken stock
2 tbsp white wine vinegar
2 tbsp olive oil
1 tbsp Dijon mustard
salt and freshly ground black pepper
1 tbsp mayonnaise
1 bunch spring onions, the whites and a bit
  of the green, finely chopped

1 Cook the new potatoes in boiling water in their skins. When tender, drain them and remove the skins if you like (but I don't).

2 Meanwhile, bring the chicken stock to the boil with the vinegar and oil. Take off the heat and stir in the mustard.

3 Immediately slice the potatoes into the hot liquor. Leave to marinate and cool, during which time the potatoes will absorb most of the liquid.

4 Season with salt and pepper, then stir in the mayonnaise and spring onion. Serve lukewarm.

Champ

SERVES 4–6

Champ is the Irish equivalent of mashed potatoes, but it includes greenery such as young leeks or kale, peas, nettles, salad or spring onions, which have been poached in milk or buttermilk. It is very similar to two other Irish dishes, boxty (see page 209) and colcannon, both of which are traditional at Hallowe'en. Colcannon often contains favours: a wedding ring for marriage, a sixpence for wealth, and a thimble and button for spinsterhood and bachelorhood respectively...

900g (2 lb) floury potatoes
salt and freshly ground black pepper
150ml (5 fl oz) buttermilk
150ml (5 fl oz) double cream
225g (8 oz) spring onions (or young leeks), finely chopped
115g (4 oz) unsalted butter

1 Wash, peel and cut the potatoes into large pieces. Cover with water, add salt and bring to the boil. Cook until tender, then strain off and return to the pan over a gentle heat to dry out. Do not colour.

2 Bring the buttermilk and double cream to the boil in a large clean pan. Add the spring onions to the milk-cream mixture, and simmer for 5 minutes. Drain off the spring onions, keeping the cream mixture.

3 Add the spring onions to the potato and mash finely. Add half the butter to the milk mixture, then beat into the potato. Season well.

4 Pour the potatoes into a serving dish and make a well in the middle. Melt the rest of the butter, pour into the well and serve immediately.

•Today people always seem to want to make things more sophisticated – turning a mixture like this into little moulds or encasing it in breadcrumbs. Let it be. The good old-fashioned way has always got to be the best.

Baked Beans

SERVES 6

A mixture of salted bacon and soaked dried beans was a dish for the poor from very early times. The Pilgrim Fathers took the idea (and the basic ingredients) to America in 1620, where the dish was adopted, adapted and developed into the famous Boston baked beans. And thereafter it was returned to us, in the form of beans canned in a tomato sauce. Such is culinary history!

450g (1 lb) dried white beans (haricots blancs)
5 garlic cloves, peeled
2 large onions, peeled and quartered
2 large carrots, trimmed and quartered
1 x 280g (10 oz) tin peeled plum tomatoes
6 medium tomatoes, skinned and seeded
salt and freshly ground black pepper

1 Soak the beans in plenty of cold water to cover for 3 hours (unless it says different on the packet).

2 Drain and put into a saucepan. Cover

with water again, bring to the boil and cook for 30 minutes.

3 Put 4 of the garlic cloves, the onions and carrots into the pot, and cook for a further hour.

4 Preheat the oven to 200°C/400°F/Gas 6.

5 Strain off the cooking liquid, and pick out and discard the vegetables and garlic.

6 Chop the tinned tomatoes, fresh tomatoes and remaining garlic clove together. Mix with the drained beans and season well. Put into an ovenproof dish with a lid.

7 Bring up to heat, put the lid on, then cook in the preheated oven for 30 minutes. Give one final check to the seasoning and serve.

•Pick through the beans for grit, stones etc., but it shouldn't be necessary these days. They shouldn't need soaking for too long either.

•Add bacon if you like, cut into strips and sautéed first.

Bubble and Squeak

SERVES 4–6

When I was a child, we always had plenty of cooked potato and cabbage left over after a meal so that we could make bubble and squeak, a classic dish for leftovers. Here, though, I describe how you might do it from scratch. Serve with cold meat, *Piccalilli* (see page 312) and/or brown sauce – and my dad used to serve it with runny fried eggs on top in his café. My own personal favourite accompaniment is black pudding...

The name 'bubble and squeak' is said to come from the noise the dish makes as it cooks, and it was originally a way of utilising leftover meat, made with meat and cabbage only. The potato addition and the gradual loss of the meat made it more like the Irish colcannon.

675g (1½ lb) medium baking potatoes, scrubbed
55g (2 oz) bacon or duck fat
450g (1 lb) Savoy cabbage, cored, finely shredded and cooked until tender
salt and freshly ground black pepper

1 Preheat the oven to 180°C/350°F/Gas 4, and bake the potatoes until tender, about an hour. Take out and leave to cool.

2 Melt the fat in an ovenproof frying pan and add the potato flesh scraped out from the potato skins, Leave until it starts to colour. Crush with a fork, but leave some lumps in.

3 Add the cooked cabbage, season with salt and pepper, and fry well, Keep moving in the pan.

4 When the bottom is coloured, put the pan in the preheated oven for 15 minutes.

•You can add other ingredients to the basic mix if you like – onions, carrots or peas, say – and you could use mashed instead of baked potato if you had that left over, or sliced cooked Brussels sprouts instead of the cabbage.

•You could shape the mixture into little cakes before frying, but why bother? It's the taste that counts and the choice of fat is *vital*.

Punchnep/Clapshot

SERVES 4–6

Outlandish names for a mixture of mashed potato and turnip or swede, the former from Wales, the latter from the Orkney Islands (where they don't tend to use cream). It is the yellow swede that is mostly used, rather than turnip, although the Welsh name reflects the 'nep' or 'turnip' connection (and swedes are actually known as turnips or 'neeps' in Scotland). Turnips, for human and animal consumption, have been around for hundreds of years, but the swede or 'Swedish turnip' was only developed in the 17th century (coming from Bohemia, not Sweden).

450g (1 lb) cooked mashed potato
350g (12 oz) cooked mashed swede
115g (4 oz) unsalted butter
salt and freshly ground black pepper
2 tbsp double cream

1 Put the cooked mashed potato and swede into a pan together and dry out over a very gentle heat. Mash together as finely as possible.

2 Beat in the butter and season with salt and pepper.

3 Put into a warm serving dish, and decorate using the flat of a warmed palette knife to make small indentations.

4 Pour the cream over the top and serve.

•Although you might think it a bit poncey to decorate the top of the potato (called 'scrolling' in the business), even my dad used to do it. He must have learned this in the Catering Corps, but he used a fish slice rather than a palette knife.

Bashed Neeps

SERVES 6-8

'Bashed neeps' (mashed *swede*, rather than turnip) and 'champit tatties' (mashed potatoes) are the classic accompaniments for the haggis eaten by the Scots at Hogmanay and on Burns Night (25 January). A nip of malt is mandatory!

The lightly spiced vegetable purée is also delicious with roast meats such as roast beef.

675g (1½ lb) swede, peeled and cut into
  even pieces
salt and freshly ground black pepper
85g (3 oz) unsalted butter
2 tbsp double cream
¼ tsp ground cinnamon
juice of ½ lemon

1 Plunge the swede pieces into boiling salted water, bring back to the boil, and cook until tender. Drain and put back into the pan.

2 Mash with a potato masher until smooth, then add the butter, cream, cinnamon and lemon juice. Season to taste and serve.

Pease Pudding

SERVES 8–10, OR 6 GREEDY PEOPLE

Dried peas used to be a staple in the diet of poor people in Britain: they were usually cooked to a porridge, perhaps along with a piece of salt bacon (good flavours still). With the invention of the pudding cloth, a more solid pudding could be made, and a round cloth ball of peas, with basic flavourings, would be boiled alongside the bacon or pork. The dish's popularity has waned a little elsewhere, but in the north of England, butchers and market stalls sell slabs of pease pudding for you to take home and reheat.

I have to admit that I'm not keen on ordinary pease pudding – or its cousin, mushy peas – but this rather richer, more sophisticated version is very tasty.

450g (1 lb) dried split peas, soaked
1 large onion, peeled and finely chopped
1 bunch each fresh thyme, parsley and
  mint
1 ham bone, or 4 bacon rashers tied
  together
600ml (1 pint) vegetable stock
salt and freshly ground black pepper
1 tbsp chopped fresh mint
1 tbsp chopped fresh parsley
60g (2¼ oz) unsalted butter
2 eggs and 1 egg yolk, beaten together

1 Strain off and put the peas into a clean pan. Add the onion and bunches of herbs, then the ham or bacon. Add the stock and then pour in enough cold water to cover. Bring to the boil, add pepper to taste, then simmer with the lid on for about an hour, or until tender.

2 Take the lid off and carefully simmer to

get rid of the rest of the liquid.

3 Take out the herbs and the ham or bacon, and discard. Put the peas into a food processor and blitz, but do not purée too much. Add the chopped fresh herbs, 55g (2 oz) of the butter and the eggs, and mix well. Check for salt especially.

4 Grease a terrine mould, loaf tin or pudding basin well with the remaining butter. Pour the pea mixture in and steam for an hour in a covered pan, or, as I prefer, bake in a bain-marie in the oven preheated to 180C/350F/Gas 4 for an hour.

5 Allow to cool, turn out, slice and serve hot or cold. You can eat straight from the dish!

Boxty Pancakes

SERVES 4

Boxty, like champ and colcannon, is one of the most famous of Ireland's potato dishes, and again like colcannon, it is traditionally made for Hallowe'en. It can be baked as a bread (see below), fried as pancakes as here, boiled as dumplings in the usual way, or boiled then sliced and fried.

450g (1 lb) large floury potatoes
225g (8 oz) plain mashed cooked potato
55g (2 oz) plain flour
½ tsp salt
1 tsp baking powder
2–4 tbsp single cream
25g (1 oz) unsalted butter, melted

To cook
unsalted butter or lard

1 Wash, peel and grate the potatoes. Put into a clean cloth, tie tightly and squeeze out all the moisture.

2 Make sure the mashed cooked potato is completely dry, and has had nothing added to it (i.e. milk, butter, cream etc.). Mix the raw grated potato and the mashed cooked potato together.

3 Sift the flour, salt and baking powder together then add to the mixture and stir well. Slowly add the cream and butter to make a sloppier mixture of a 'drop-pancake' (scone) consistency.

4 Heat a griddle or a heavy frying pan. Use butter for sweet pancakes, i.e. if served with treacle etc., or lard when served with something like bacon. Use three large 7.5cm (3 in) metal rings to help keep a uniform shape.

5 Drop the mixture into the rings in the frying pan to about 5mm (¼ in) thickness. Allow to set and colour golden brown. Take the rings off, and turn the pancakes over. Cook them through, a few more minutes until golden, and keep warm while you make the remainder.

•To make into a bread mix, leave out the cream and use a little milk instead. Knead well, shape into a round and bake in the oven preheated to 180°C/350°F/Gas 4 for 35–40 minutes.

Cauliflower Cheese

SERVES 4

Cauliflowers, which belong to the cabbage family, were developed by the Arabs, and in the eighteenth century in Britain were highly regarded vegetables, suitable for the best treatment, being buttered, coated with a rich white sauce and sprinkled with cheese. It's thought of more now as a supper or high tea dish, on a par with macaroni cheese, but cooked well, it can be great. My grandmother wouldn't recognise the modern additions of Parmesan and breadcrumbs, but they are worthwhile, adding both flavour and texture.

1 large cauliflower
salt and freshly ground black pepper
55g (2 oz) Parmesan, freshly grated
1 tbsp white breadcrumbs

Cheese sauce
40g (1½ oz) unsalted butter
40g (1½ oz) plain flour
300ml (10 fl oz) double cream
150ml (5 fl oz) milk
a dash of Tabasco sauce
1 tsp Dijon mustard
175g (6 oz) Lancashire cheese, grated

1 Preheat the oven to 180°C/350°F/Gas 4.

2 Cut the cauliflower into even-sized florets. Plunge these into boiling salted water and cook until tender, then drain (keep the water).

3 Meanwhile, for the cheese sauce, melt the butter in a medium pan. add the flour and cook for 2 minutes, stirring to avoid lumps. Add the cream and bring back to the boil, still stirring. Add the milk, whisk in and take from the heat. Add the Tabasco and mustard and stir in well, along with the Lancashire cheese. Season to taste. If the sauce is a little thick, add 2 tbsp of the cauliflower water.

4 Arrange the cooked florets of cauliflower in a dish, if possible built to look like a whole cauliflower. Gently pour the sauce over.

5 Sprinkle with the Parmesan and bread-crumbs and bake in the preheated oven for 15 minutes until brown on top. Serve immediately.

•A tendency these days is to undercook cauliflower for this dish. But, although you don't want it to be a mush or purée, it should be soft enough to be able to spoon out easily (soft enough for your grandma to eat without her teeth!).

•Another way of cooking the cauli would be to gouge out the centre stalk, leaving the vegetable whole with a hole in the middle. Cook it for a little longer to ensure the inside parts are cooked.

•Much as I hate to admit it, in my tests the acidity and crumbliness of Lancashire cheese worked better than a Yorkshire Wensleydale (But if you can't get either, a Cheddar will do fine.)

Brussels Sprouts with Chestnuts

SERVES 4

Brussels sprouts were developed in the Low Countries in the Middle Ages, but did not become popular in Britain until the mid-nineteenth century (and are still not particularly popular in some quarters...) Chestnuts too have been with us for ever, although the French and the Italians have always appreciated them rather more in a culinary sense. The combination of the two is fairly recent, I imagine, created probably because both are in season at the same time.

Although now traditional with our Christmas turkey, the vegetable mixture is so good it deserves to be used more often – delicious with roast pork or poultry, for instance.

225g (8 oz) chestnuts
350g (12 oz) Brussels sprouts
salt and freshly ground black pepper
55g (2 oz) unsalted butter

1 Make a cross with a small sharp knife in the bottom of each chestnut and cook in the preheated oven for 20 minutes or until the shells start to split. Cool a little until you can handle them, then peel.

2 Meanwhile, prepare the Brussels. Trim off the outside leaves and put a cross in the stalk of each. Plunge into boiling salted water and cook until just done. Refresh and drain.

3 Cut the peeled chestnuts and the cooked sprouts in half. Fry in the butter to heat through and brown a little, then season and serve.

•You could cook the dish in an interesting alternative way. Shred the sprouts before cooking. Stir-fry in butter, add some chopped garlic to taste and the cooked, peeled and crumbled chestnuts. Season and serve.

•The best chestnuts are those cooked in a special container over an open fire. To test whether a chestnut is ready, shell one, dip it in salt and eat. You'll soon know. (And be sure to buy more chestnuts than you need if, like me. you are obliged to carry on testing to see whether they are ready...)

Laverbread with Bacon

SERVES 4

Laver is an edible seaweed which is found on coastlines mainly in the west of Britain, in Wales, Scotland and Ireland (known as 'sloke' in the last two countries). It is gathered, washed and boiled for several hours until it is like a dark-green spinach purée. This is when it is known as 'laverbread' in Wales, where laver is most commonly eaten still. It is served on toast, dressed as a salad, or mixed with oatmeal to make laver cakes, which are fried in bacon fat. I have taken the basic cake idea a little further here. Apparently laver was once mixed with orange juice to make a sauce for roast lamb and mutton.

Laver is known as *nori* in Japan, where it is cultivated. It is mainly available in dried sheets, and in this form has become very much more fashionable than poor old laver, as a wrapping for sushi and similar foods.

225g (8 oz) cooked laver
350g (12 oz) plain mashed cooked potato
25g (1 oz) unsalted butter, melted

salt and freshly ground black pepper
freshly grated nutmeg
4 rashers streaky bacon
225g (8 oz) oatmeal
55g (2 oz) lard
8 rashers smoked back bacon

1 Mix the laver and mashed potato together. Stir in the butter and season with salt, pepper and nutmeg. Leave to stand for a few minutes.

2 Cook the streaky bacon until crisp in a hot pan, and then chop into small dice. Mix into the laver mixture along with half of the oatmeal.

3 Mould into four balls of about 115g (4 oz) each. Roll in the remaining oatmeal and flatten into cakes to look like fishcakes.

4 Fry in the hot lard until golden brown, then turn over and cook through. Meanwhile, cook the smoked bacon.

5 Serve the laver cakes with the rashers of bacon over them.

Braised Leeks

SERVES 4

Leeks have been valued since the time of the ancients. The Emperor Nero apparently ate them in an attempt to improve his singing voice! Everyone grew leeks at one time, as they were a pot (pottage) vegetable, and many towns are actually named after the 'leac-tun', or leek enclosure (such as Leighton). Leeks went into a decline in a fashionable sense, but in the furthest parts of Britain, in Ireland, Scotland and Wales – especially the latter, where it's the national symbol – it survived in many classic recipes. The Welsh make leek pies and braise them, the Scots use them in *Cock-a-Leekie* (see page 19), and the Irish use them in *Champ* (see page 199).

Most traditional leek recipes have them boiled or braised in butter. I have refined the braising idea a little, which gives good flavour. The leeks are good with any roast meats, particularly lamb and duck.

900g (2 lb) young leeks
salt and freshly ground black pepper

unsalted butter
1 onion, peeled
1 carrot, trimmed
2 celery stalks, trimmed
1 tbsp fresh thyme leaves
300ml (10 fl oz) chicken or vegetable stock
1 tsp fécule (potato flour) or cornflour, slaked in 1 tbsp water

1 Preheat the oven to 180°C/350°F/Gas 4.

2 Trim the leeks of their roots and cut away the dark green tops in a pointed 'v' shape. Wash well, turning them upside down under running water.

3 Plunge the leeks into boiling salted water and cook for 5 minutes, then run under cold water to refresh.

4 Butter a suitably sized ovenproof dish. Chop the vegetables into small dice and put into the dish, along with the thyme.

5 Squeeze excess moisture from each leek. Tap halfway up with a knife and fold in half. Lay on top of the diced vegetables and pour over the stock.

6 Cover with buttered greaseproof paper and cook in the preheated oven for 45

minutes. Take the leeks out of the cooking dish and put into a serving dish, Keep warm.

7 Strain the liquor, discarding the vegetables. Reduce the liquor by one-third and thicken with the slaked fécule or cornflour. Add 25g (1 oz) butter to the sauce, season, then pour over the leeks and serve.

•You don't have to discard the braising vegetables, although they will have given most of their flavour to the liquor. Simply leave the leeks and veg in the dish and pour the sauce over all.

•Celery, chicory and other vegetables could be cooked in the same way. You could also sprinkle some grated cheese on the top and brown under the grill at the last moment.

Broad Bean and Bacon Salad

SERVES 4

Before the great explorations of the sixteenth century, we only had the broad bean in Europe, and it would have played a huge part in the diet, being eaten fresh in the summer (pods and all at first, as is becoming popular among fashionable gardeners), then dried for winter use. Dried beans and bacon was a common combination from the very earliest times, and I have brought the idea up to date, using fresh beans instead in a starter salad.

900g (2 lb) broad beans in their pods
salt and freshly ground black pepper
4 rashers back bacon, finely diced
4½ tbsp olive oil
2 tomatoes, skinned and seeded
1 shallot, peeled
½ tsp French mustard
1 tbsp white wine vinegar
1 garlic clove, peeled
1 tbsp chopped mixed fresh parsley, chervil and tarragon

To serve
about 55g (2 oz) mixed salad leaves

1 Remove the beans from their pods. Plunge into boiling salted water and simmer for 10 minutes or until tender. Remove, refresh in cold water and drain.

2 If the 'inner' grey skins are tough (more likely in larger and older beans), remove these skins with your thumb and forefinger to reveal the bright green insides, being careful not to crush them.

3 Meanwhile, fry the bacon in ½ tbsp of the olive oil until brown and crisp, Remove from the heat. Cut the tomato flesh into small dice and finely chop the shallot.

4 Mix the shallot with the mustard and then the wine vinegar. Crush the garlic and add to the bacon. Toss and put into a serving bowl with the shallot and mustard mixture.

5 Add the remaining olive oil, and the beans and herbs. Mix and season to taste with salt and pepper. Leave for 30 minutes to marinate and cool.

6 To serve, present on a small bed of mixed leaves, making sure the beans and their dressing coat the leaves. Finish off with a good grinding of black pepper.

7

Puddings

Monsieur Misson, a French visitor to England in the 1690s, wrote about the English penchant for puddings. 'Ah, what an excellent thing is an English pudding! To come in pudding-time, is as much as to say, to come in the most lucky moment in the world.' What he was so enthusiastically referring to was mainly the pudding which was made with a mixture of suet or marrow, flour, dried fruits, spices and sugar. This would have been stuffed into an animal gut, and boiled in water, either alone, or with other foods such as meat. These guts were available when the animals were slaughtered, in the autumn, thus his reference to 'pudding-time'. With the invention of the pudding cloth or bag, though, puddings could be made at any time of year. The pudding was the carbohydrate part of a meal, but was not served as a separate course: that came later. Steamed puds, such as spotted dick, Snowdon pudding and jam roly-poly – and indeed Christmas pudding – are current examples of these early puddings.

Gradually the word 'pudding' came to refer to other sweet things, and specifically to sweet things that were served as a separate course at the end of a meal. Many of the other 'sweet things' had as long a heritage as the steamed or boiled pudding. Rice puddings and other grain and milk puddings are an echo of the medieval grain dishes known as 'frumenty', simply using imported ingredients instead of local. Egg custards were popular in the Middle Ages, and they are used in many famous puddings. Bread and butter pudding (now so ubiquitous I didn't think you needed another one here!), apple charlotte and queen of puddings also illustrate another consistent strand in British puddings, the use of bread and breadcrumbs.

But it is perhaps our sweet pies for which we are most famous: our plate pies with one or two layers of pastry, our deep-dish pies, flans, tarts, turnovers and pasties. And there are a host of other fruit puddings with or without pastry, among them apple crumble (well, the crumble topping is *almost* pastry) and the more recent, but famous summer pudding (where bread is used *instead* of pastry). And a final strand represented here is that of the cold creamy puddings such as syllabubs, trifles and fools. They were thought to be less important than other courses in the meal, so all gained rather silly names...

Apple Pie

SERVES 4

This must be the most ancient of British apple puddings, a layer of apple between two layers of pastry. This was a medieval idea (taken by the Pilgrim Fathers to America), and it seems to have survived particularly in the north of England. Elsewhere an apple pie usually has a pastry top only (a pastry *bottom* in France), but plate fruit pies are still made in Yorkshire, Lancashire and further north. This is my father's recipe, which he served in his café, often mixing the apple with blackberries, raspberries or (tinned) cherries. My gran used to serve it with Wensleydale cheese: 'Apple pie without cheese is like a kiss without a squeeze.'

Pastry
225g (8 oz) plain flour
3½ tsp salt
25g (1 oz) unrefined caster sugar, plus
  extra for sprinkling
finely grated zest of 1 orange and 1 lemon
85g (3 oz) cold unsalted butter, diced
85g (3 oz) cold lard, diced

about 3 tbsp cold water to mix
1 egg mixed with a little water for egg wash

Filling
450g (1 lb) cooking apples
55g (2 oz) unrefined caster sugar
55g (2 oz) liquid honey

1 To make the pastry, sift the flour and salt together, then add the sugar and lemon and orange zests. With cold fingertips, carefully rub in the butter and lard until like breadcrumbs. Add only enough water to pull it together to a dough. Wrap in clingfilm and put aside to rest for 30 minutes.

2 Peel and core the apples, and cut them into large chunks. Add the sugar and honey and leave to stand for 20 minutes.

3 Meanwhile, preheat the oven to 200°C/400°F/Gas 6.

4 Use a third of the pastry and roll it out into a round shape to fit your chosen non-stick ovenproof pie plate (they used to be enamel). Start with a ball of pastry, it's easier. Lightly grease the oven plate.

5 Lay the pastry gently on the greased plate and pile in the apple mixture. Brush around the edges with egg wash.

6 Roll out the remaining pastry again from a ball shape to a round which will fit over the mounded tart. Put in place and pat down to seal roughly. Trim around the outside and firmly 'crimp' the edges. Brush with the remaining egg wash, sprinkle with sugar, and cut a hole in the centre for the steam to escape.

7 Bake in the preheated oven for 15 minutes, then turn the temperature down to 180°C/350°F/Gas 4 and bake for a further 20–25 minutes.

8 When out of the oven, dredge with caster sugar and serve hot, with clotted cream, crème Chantilly, ice-cream (as they did at Simpson's in the Strand) or *Custard Sauce* (see page 332) – or a combination of the whole lot!

•You can add spices to the basic apple filling. Cloves are traditional, and I remember one particular occasion when I was at college being taught how to make a deep apple pie. Being a smartie pants, I read the recipe very quickly and, without thinking, chopped up a clove of garlic, and included it in my pie. When mine was ready and the tutor was tasting it, I had to think quickly, having already realised my mistake.

'Sorry, sir, I must have forgotten to wash my knife.'

•Raisins and sultanas can also be added. In fact, there are no end of variations possible.

Bakewell Tart

SERVES 8

Another pudding which includes a layer of jam (see *Queen of Puddings*, page 249), Bakewell tart was originally known as Bakewell pudding and still is in parts of Derbyshire today. There are several stories about how it came into existence, but most are apocryphal as it has long been known in its present form – a pastry case with a jam lining and an almond 'cake' topping. This almond mixture is known as 'frangipane' in the business, and I always wondered what the connection between it and the flower, frangipani, was. It seems a trifle tenuous, but the almond mix was supposedly named after an Italian aristocrat, Frangipani, who invented a perfume, probably using red jasmine, or frangipani, for the gloves of Louis XIII...

Pastry
175g (6 oz) plain flour
a pinch of salt
25g (1 oz) unrefined caster sugar
finely grated zest of 1 orange and 1 lemon
55g (2 oz) cold unsalted butter, diced
25g (1 oz) cold lard, diced
about 2 tbsp ice-cold water to mix

Filling
55g (2 oz) raspberry jam
3 eggs
115g (4 oz) unrefined caster sugar
115g (4 oz) unsalted butter, melted
115g (4 oz) ground almonds
25g (1 oz) icing sugar, mixed with a little
    water to a thin icing

1 Make the pastry as in the recipe on page 232, adding the finely grated citrus zests, and put it aside to rest for about 20 minutes.

2 Meanwhile, preheat the oven to 180°C/350°F/Gas 4.

3 Roll the pastry out to a round to fit a 25cm (10 in) flan ring, and place in the ring. Cut off any excess pastry, and crimp the edges.

4 Warm the jam and then, if you can be

bothered (but it's the correct way), press it through a fine sieve to get rid of the seeds. Spread over the base of the tart.

5 Meanwhile, beat the eggs and sugar together, and then slowly fold in the melted butter and the ground almonds. Pour carefully into the pastry-lined flan ring.

6 Bake in the preheated oven until set, about 35 minutes. Take out and cool.

7 Pour the icing into the centre of the tart and, using a palette knife, spread it as thinly as possible. Leave to set.

Treacle Tart

SERVES 4

Treacle tart must be the quintessential British pudding – a pastry base filled with bread, eggs and sugar. It's made all over Britain, from Scotland (where a huge amount of sugar came in from the West Indies) down to Yorkshire. Sometimes the tart is actually a plate pie (top and bottom pastry); often it is a plate tart, but with interwoven pastry strips decorating the top.

Here I have made little individual tarts with only one layer of pastry. Whatever you do, it is an unadulterated sweet delight.

250g (9 oz) *Sweet Pastry* (see page 232)

Filling
25g (1 oz) fine fresh breadcrumbs
275g (9½ oz) golden syrup
juice and finely grated zest of 1 lemon
1 tbsp dark treacle
3 eggs

1 Roll out the sweet pastry and use to line four 10cm (4 in) round, non-stick tart moulds, 2cm (¾ in) deep. Rest in the fridge for half an hour.

2 Meanwhile, preheat the oven to 180°C/350°F/Gas 4.

3 For the filling, mix together the breadcrumbs, syrup, treacle, lemon juice and zest.

4 Beat the eggs, then add to the breadcrumb mixture.

5 Pour the filling into the pastry-lined moulds and bake in the preheated oven for 15–20 minutes. Serve warm with clotted cream.

Lemon Meringue Pie

SERVES 8

Fruit tarts and fruit cheese or curd tarts are long-standing elements of British cooking, but the meringue topping, possibly an American influence – they have 'chiffon' pies – dates from much later. There are several other puds which use a meringue topping – butterscotch tart, Oxford and Cambridge pudding, a Welsh border tart – and, of course, *Queen of Puddings* (see page 249).

Sweet pastry
225g (8 oz) plain flour
a pinch of salt
25g (1 oz) unrefined caster sugar
115g (4 oz) cold unsalted butter
2 egg yolks, beaten
approx. 2 tbsp water

Lemon filling
4 juicy lemons
150ml (5 fl oz) water
55g (2 oz) unsalted butter
85g (3 oz) unrefined caster sugar

25g (1 oz) cornflour, slaked in a little water
3 egg yolks

Meringue topping
3 egg whites
a pinch of salt
115g (4 oz) unrefined caster sugar
icing sugar

1 To make the pastry, sift the flour and salt into a bowl and add the sugar. Chop the cold butter and rub into the flour until the texture resembles breadcrumbs. Add the egg yolks. Mix to a dough, using the water if necessary, and form into a ball. If you have time, chill, wrapped in clingfilm, for about 20 minutes.

2 Roll the pastry dough out to a circle of about 33cm (13 in) to line the base and sides of a 25cm (10 in) flan ring. Place the flan ring on a baking sheet and line with the pastry circle. Neaten the edges, and leave to rest in the fridge for half an hour.

3 Meanwhile, preheat the oven to 180°C/350°F/Gas 4.

4 Fill the pastry casing with a circle of greaseproof paper and fill with beans or rice. Bake in the preheated oven for 15 minutes. Take out of the oven, remove the beans and paper, and reduce the oven temperature to 140°C/275°F/Gas 1. Bake for 10 more minutes. Remove and turn the oven temperature up to 160°C/325°F/Gas 3.

5 Meanwhile, for the lemon filling, zest two of the lemons into a saucepan. Squeeze all four lemons into the pan and add the water, the butter and sugar, and bring to the boil.

6 Add the slaked cornflour, bring up to the boil again and gently stir until thickened.

7 Beat the egg yolks together, then pour a little sauce on to them. Stir in and then pour back into the pan. Gently heat and stir – do not boil – for 2 minutes. Pour into the flan case.

8 Meanwhile, for the meringue topping, whisk the egg whites to peaks with the salt, then add 25g (1 oz) of sugar at a time, continually whisking, until all the sugar has been whisked in.

9 Spoon the meringue over the pie and use the back of the spoon to make random peaks. Sprinkle with a little icing sugar.

10 Bake the pie in the preheated oven for 25 minutes. Take out, sprinkle with more icing sugar and leave to cool. Eat cold.

•Any citrus fruit will work – oranges, grapefruit, mandarins – but always check for the quantity of juice. I actually worry a little about giving fruit for juice in numbers: at certain times you might need ten fruit to get the same amount of juice as from four juicier ones at a different time.

•If you want to be really posh, you could use a piping bag to put the meringue on.

Spotted Dick

SERVES 4–6

Perhaps the most infamous of British roly-poly puddings – and not just the cause of many a schoolboy snigger: recently an English health service board was forced to rescind its decision to re-christen the pudding 'Spotted Richard' on hospital menus, with a well-known supermarket chain following suit... It is also known as spotted dog (strictly speaking, when the dried fruit is mixed *with* the pastry instead of being encased in it) and plum bolster.

225g (8 oz) plain flour, plus extra for
  sprinkling
15g (½ oz) baking powder
a pinch of salt
115g (4 oz) finely chopped beef suet
150ml (5 fl oz) water
115g (4 oz) currants
55g (2 oz) raisins
grated zest of 1 lemon

1 To make the basic suet pastry, sift the flour, baking powder and salt together, then rub in the suet. Add the water and mix to a dough.

2 Roll out to a rectangle 25 x 15cm (10 x 6in) and 1cm (½in) thick. Sprinkle with the currants and raisins, leaving a border of 1cm (½in) round all sides. Press the fruit in and sprinkle with the lemon zest. Paint the borders with water.

3 Turn the two short sides in and seal. Roll up from a long side carefully, to keep all the fruit in. Seal when rolled up.

4 Rinse a clean tea towel in boiling water. Sprinkle with flour and shake off the excess. Lay the roll on top of the cloth, fold the cloth over and fix at the ends with string. Steam the cloth-wrapped roll for 1½ hours. Or you could put the pud on a rack in a roasting tray full of water, then cover it with foil. Bring to the boil then steam in the oven at 200°C/400°F/Gas 6 for about 2 hours. Top up the water occasionally. Or bake at the above oven temperature, but not in the cloth, brushed with egg wash, for about 1½ hours.

5 Take out, unwrap while still hot (if necessary), cut into slices and serve with *Custard Sauce* (see page 332) or jam sauce.

Snowdon Pudding

SERVES 6

This Welsh suet pudding is made in the classic way, but with a few characteristic differences. The raisins and marmalade form a light coating around the rest of the pudding mix, and the white cream sauce, poured on at the end, looks like the snow that often lies on the top of Snowdon during winter.

25g (1 oz) unsalted butter
115g (4 oz) raisins
2 tbsp orange marmalade
115g (4 oz) chopped beef suet
175g (6 oz) fresh white breadcrumbs

1 tbsp ground rice
2 tbsp orange marmalade
finely grated zest of 1 orange
finely grated zest of 1 lemon
55g (2 oz) unrefined caster sugar
2 eggs

Sauce
85g (3 oz) unrefined caster sugar
juice of 1 lemon
150ml (5 fl oz) dry white wine
150ml (5 fl oz) double cream

1 Blitz the butter and raisins together in the blender, then push through a sieve. Brush the inside of a 1.2 litre (2 pint) pudding basin with this mixture, and then put the marmalade in the bottom of the pudding basin.

2 Mix all the other pudding ingredients together and put into the basin. Cover with greased greaseproof paper and a pudding cloth and tie tightly. Steam for 1½ hours.

3 Meanwhile, for the cream sauce, boil the sugar, lemon juice and white wine together to reduce by two-thirds. Add the double cream and boil to thicken.

4 To serve, turn the pudding out and pour the sauce over.

Sticky Toffee Pudding

SERVES 8

Dried fruit boiled in a suet pastry base in a cloth would once have been the most traditional British pudding. As ovens became more common, the pastry base became lighter, and here the fruit is mixed with a darkly sweet cake mixture. Francis Coulson and Brian Sack of the Sharrow Bay Hotel in Cumbria were responsible, I think, for reintroducing us to the joys of this pudding.

175g (6 oz) medjool dates
115g (4 oz) dried figs
55g (2 oz) sultanas
150ml (5 fl oz) boiling water
finely grated zest of 2 oranges
115g (4 oz) unsalted butter
175g (6 oz) unrefined demerara sugar
3 eggs, beaten
140g (5 oz) self-raising flour
55g (2 oz) ground almonds
55g (2 oz) pistachio nuts, chopped

Sauce
115g (4 oz) unsalted butter

175g (6 oz) unrefined demerara sugar
150ml (5 fl oz) double cream

1 Grease a baking tray about 20cm (8 in) square, or the same volume, and preheat the oven to 180°C/350°F/Gas 4.

2 Stone the dates and chop them finely with the figs and sultanas. Put them into a bowl and pour the boiling water over. Whisk to a pulp, then add the orange zest.

3 Cream the butter and sugar together then add the egg. Beat together, then fold in the flour, ground almonds and fruit pulp.

4 Pour the mixture into the prepared baking tray and bake in the preheated oven for 30–40 minutes. To test if cooked, press with your hand: there will be some resistance. Take out when cooked and allow to cool slightly.

5 Cut the cooled cake into shapes. I like round ones, although this means wastage: use a round metal cutter (the leftover bits could possibly be used in one of the other puddings in the book). Squares mean you can use the whole thing!

6 Meanwhile, for the sauce, melt the butter, add the sugar and bring to the boil.

Add the double cream and simmer for 5 minutes until lightly thickened.

7 Pour a little sauce over and around the pudding, sprinkle with the chopped pistachios and serve.

Rice Pudding

SERVES 8

A cereal 'pottage', a semi liquid cooked dish, was everyday fare for rich and poor alike from the Middle Ages all over the country. In the north they would use oats (and 'porridge' is the dish still most similar to the medieval pottage), in the south, rye, barley and wheat. When rice was (expensively) introduced from Italy, it was mixed with milk and sweet spices and baked or boiled. Sometimes eggs were added for a richer result, and in Yorkshire, suet was often included as well. Our present-day rice puddings are not too different from these early originals. Whether they liked the skin then or not, I don't know...

55g (2 oz) Carolina short-grain rice
450ml (15 fl oz) milk

150ml (5 fl oz) double cream
55g (2 oz) unrefined caster sugar
1 vanilla pod
25g (1 oz) unsalted butter
freshly grated nutmeg

1 Put the rice, milk and cream into a thick-bottomed pan and bring to the boil, stirring all the time.

2 Add the sugar, the seeds from the vanilla pod and the pod itself. Simmer until cooked, stirring regularly, about 45–50 minutes, Remove the pod.

3 Add the butter and nutmeg to taste, then pour into a dish and colour the top under the preheated grill until golden brown.

4 Serve with freshly made, whole fruit *Strawberry Jam* (see page 313).

•For a slightly fancier version, you could add a couple of eggs. When the rice is cooked, butter a pie dish. Beat 2 egg yolks into the rice. Whisk 2 egg whites and then fold them into the rice. Spoon into the pie dish and bake in the preheated oven at 160°C/325°F/Gas 3 for 15-20 minutes. Sprinkle with icing sugar and serve.

Apple and Pineapple Crumble

SERVES 6

Although we have long loved fruit pies using pastry, fruit with a crumble topping – basically sweet pastry ingredients without the water – is very much more recent. Some suggest it did not come into use until after World War Two, perhaps when sugar had stopped being rationed. And of course a crumble is much easier and quicker to make than a pastry! The idea may have come from the Austrian 'streusel', a cake topping which, because it contains less flour, bakes to a crisper texture than our distinctly crumbly crumble.

25g (1 oz) unsalted butter
350g (12 oz) eating apples
225g (8 oz) fresh peeled pineapple
85g (3 oz) unrefined caster sugar

Crumble topping
115g (4 oz) cold unsalted butter, diced
225g (8 oz) plain flour
115g (4 oz) unrefined demerara sugar

1 Preheat the oven to 180°C/350°F/Gas 4.

Butter a pie dish generously.

2 Peel and core the apples and cut into 1cm (½ in) dice. Cut the fresh pineapple to the same size and mix with the apple. Put into the buttered pie dish and pat down. Sprinkle the caster sugar over to form a flat bed.

3 To make the crumble topping, rub the cold butter dice into the flour to form a breadcrumb-like mixture. Stir in the demerara sugar then sprinkle some of this over the fruit. Pat down firmly, then sprinkle the rest on top.

4 Bake in the preheated oven for 15 minutes. Turn the oven temperature down to 160°C/325°F/Gas 3 and bake until well coloured, about another 25 minutes.

5 Serve with *Custard Sauce* (see page 332) or ice-cream.

•Apple and blackberry crumble is probably more familiar, but pineapple is a good foil for the apple. (And, although it is not very British, it has actually been enthusiastically grown in English hothouses since the seventeenth century. The pineapples which adorn iron railings and gates from that period are proof of its popularity and familiarity.)

Apple Charlotte

SERVES 4

Although the pudding itself is a typical British combination of home-grown apples and bread (in this case fried), the name 'charlotte' has been the subject of some debate over the years. It is most likely that the pud was christened in honour of the wife of George III, Charlotte Sophia of Mecklenburg-Strelitz, in the late eighteenth century. This pudding is baked, but later the famous French chef, Carême, invented a cold version, the Charlotte Russe, when the mould was lined with sponge fingers instead of bread.

approx. 12 slices day-old bread
55g (2 oz) clarified butter (see page 80), melted
450g (1 lb) cooking apples
55g (2 oz) unsalted butter
11g (4 oz) unrefined caster sugar
1 cinnamon stick
finely grated zest of 1 lemon
juice of ½ lemon
55g (2 oz) fresh white breadcrumbs
icing sugar and clotted cream to serve

1 Take the crusts off the bread. Cut the bread out to line a 1.2 litre (2 pint) pie dish (or four individual ramekins).

2 Fry the bread quickly in the clarified butter, to brown only on one side. Lay the fried bread in the base and then round the sides of the dish, rather as you would for summer pudding, brown side down and outside.

3 Preheat the oven to 180°C/350°F/Gas 4.

4 Meanwhile, peel, core and quarter the apples. Put half of them into a pan with the butter, sugar, cinnamon, lemon zest and juice. Cook until the apples start to pulp, then add the rest. Cook for 5 more minutes, then add the breadcrumbs.

5 Pour this mixture into the pie dish and cover with more bread slices to seal the apples in. Bake in the preheated oven for 40–50 minutes.

6 Take out of the oven and leave to cool for 5 minutes only. Turn out, dredge with icing sugar and serve with clotted cream.

•You could use brioche instead of bread, and pears instead of apples.

Summer Pudding

SERVES 4–6

The British pudding tradition is long established, but the word 'pudding' is most commonly associated with cooked and hot – suet puds, baked batter, pastry and milk puds. Summer pudding, however, is a later invention, and although the fruit is heated slightly to render the juices, it is basically uncooked and it is served cold. The concept of fruit encased in bread rather than pastry came into being in the eighteenth century, created for patients not permitted the richness of pastry. For some time it was actually known as hydropathic pudding, after the sanatoria where the selfsame patients were being treated.

900g (2 lb) mixed summer fruits
(blackberries, raspberries, bilberries,
 redcurrants, blackcurrants)
115g (4 oz) unrefined caster sugar
1 cinnamon stick
juice of 1 lemon
approx. 450g (1 lb) day-old, medium
 sliced bread

1 Clean the fruit and put into a pan. Add the sugar, cinnamon stick and lemon juice, bring up to the boil and simmer gently for 5 minutes.

2 Gently strain off the fruit – a colander works well – and keep the fruit to one side. Reduce the juices by half by boiling, then allow to cool.

3 Take the crusts off the bread and cut a circle from each slice to fit the bottom of four to six ramekin dishes. Cut the same number of circles for the tops as well. Cut the rest of the bread into wedges to fit the walls of the ramekins. It is important that there are no gaps in the bread: to overlap is better.

4 Dip the circles for the base into the reduced juices, and then put into the ramekins. Dip the bread for the sides into the juice and place around the sides. Fill the ramekins with the fruit, then lay the second circle on top. Put a piece of greaseproof paper on top and a light weight on top of that in turn to press it down. Refrigerate overnight.

5 Turn out and serve with clotted cream and a pool of the juice.

•For an exciting alternative, use brioche loaf instead of ordinary bread.

Queen of Puddings

SERVES 6

This old fashioned pudding combines two major strands of the British pudding tradition. The baked custard is one, and the use of bread is another. The jam is fairly characteristic too, but the meringue was a later, probably foreign addition (and which features in many other traditional sweets, such as *Lemon Meringue Pie*, see page 232).

However, having said all that, I've used cake crumbs here instead of breadcrumbs, which just refines the idea a little. In fact you could use any cake, really, even chocolate, as a good way of using up those last wedges that no-one wants. And, of course, instead of using a lattice meringue you could always simply spread the meringue over the top with a palette knife.

300ml (10 fl oz) milk
300ml (10 fl oz) double cream
1 vanilla pod, split
4 eggs, separated

140g (5 oz) unrefined caster sugar
finely grated zest of 1 lemon
freshly grated nutmeg
55g (2 oz) unsalted butter
115g (4 oz) plain sponge cake crumbs
55g (2 oz) raspberry jam, warmed and
  strained

To decorate
glacé cherries
angelica
icing sugar

1 Put the milk and cream into a suitable saucepan, and scrape in the vanilla seeds. Add the pod and bring the mixture just to the boil.

2 Beat the egg yolks and 55g (2 oz) of the sugar together in a bowl. Pour the cream mixture over the eggs and sugar, then add the lemon zest and nutmeg to taste.

3 Grease a pie dish with the butter, and put the cake crumbs into it. Pour the sauce over and leave for 20 minutes. Remove the vanilla pod.

4 Meanwhile, preheat the oven to 180°C/350°F/Gas 4.

5 Bake the custard in the preheated oven

until set, about 20 minutes. Take out and leave to set for 5 minutes, then spread the warmed raspberry jam over.

6 Warm the remaining sugar slightly in the oven, no more than 5 minutes. Take out when it feels just warm to the touch.

7 For the meringue topping, whisk the egg whites to firm, and then whisk in the warmed sugar. Put in a piping bag and pipe lattice style round and over the top.

8 Decorate (like a crown) with cherries and angelica, then dredge with icing sugar and put back in the oven to brown and set the meringue, about 10–15 minutes. Serve warm.

•Slit your vanilla pod in half lengthways, and scrape out the seeds from both halves with the blade of a knife. The seeds hold the most intense flavour, but you should always use the pod as well.

Cabinet Pudding

SERVES 6

A relative of many other British custard puddings, this one can be either baked and served hot as here, or made to be served cold. It also varies in title, being known variously as cabinet, diplomat and chancellor's pudding. Why the political connection I don't know, but it's a good rib-sticking winter warmer.

55g (2 oz) unsalted butter
300ml (10 fl oz) milk
150ml (5 fl oz) double cream
1 vanilla pod
2 eggs plus 3 egg yolks
55g (2 oz) unrefined caster sugar
55g (2 oz) muscatel sultanas
25g (1 oz) glacé cherries
25g (1 oz) angelica
175g (6 oz) sponge cake, diced
finely grated zest of 2 lemons
150ml (5 fl oz) brandy

1 Using all the butter grease a medium-sized pie dish (or small moulds).

2 Put the milk and double cream on to a gentle heat. Scrape the vanilla seeds from the pod and put into the milk, along with the pod.

3 Beat the eggs and yolks well together with the sugar.

4 Chop the dried fruits finely, then sprinkle half of them on to the base of the pie dish. Mix the sponge cake with the rest of the fruit and the lemon zest, and pile into the pie dish. Pour the brandy over and leave for 5 minutes.

5 Pour the heated milk over the beaten eggs and sugar and stir in well. Take the pod out and pour half of the custard over the cake. Leave for 5 minutes.

6 Meanwhile, preheat the oven to 180°C/350°F/Gas 4.

7 Pour the rest of the custard on top of the dish and bake in the preheated oven in a bain-marie of warm water for 20 minutes. Turn the temperature down to 160°C/325°F/Gas 3 and cook for another 20 minutes.

8 Take out of the oven and allow to stand

for 5 minutes. Turn out and serve hot, with a jam sauce perhaps. Also good cold with ice-cream.

•Instead of the sponge cake, you could use soaked sponge fingers, macaroons or ratafia biscuits.

Chocolate and Raspberry Trifle

SERVES 4

One of the most famous cold British desserts, the trifle has changed in nature over the years. Originally it consisted of wine-soaked almond biscuits, covered with custard, then topped with *Syllabub* (page 256). When I was a child, trifle was made in a posh crystal bowl. The jelly was out of a packet, fruit out of a tin, sponge out of a packet, and custard out of a tin. If you were lucky, it was topped with cream out of a cow. When you put your spoon in, it made a noise that made Gran look askance... This is my version!

175g (6 oz) white chocolate
2 egg yolks
25g (1 oz) unrefined caster sugar

150ml (5 fl oz) milk
85ml (3 fl oz) double cream
2½ tbsp icing sugar
4 x 4cm (1½in) slices Swiss roll
2 tbsp Kirsch liqueur
225g (8 oz) fresh raspberries
a few sprigs fresh mint

1 Put a 55g (2 oz) piece of the white chocolate in the fridge; this will make it easier to grate later. Break the remainder into small pieces.

2 Cream the egg yolks and sugar together in a large bowl. Whisk for about 2–3 minutes until the mixture is pale, thick, creamy and leaves a trail.

3 Pour the milk and cream into a small, heavy-based saucepan and bring to the boil. Pour on to the egg yolk mixture, whisking all the time. Pour back into the pan and place over a moderate heat. Stir the mixture with a wooden spoon until it starts to thicken and coats the back of the spoon. Add the broken-up pieces of chocolate and stir in until completely incorporated. Remove the pan from the heat and allow to cool slightly. Cover the custard with a little icing sugar and a piece of clingfilm to prevent a skin forming.

4 Place the Swiss roll slices in a large glass bowl and sprinkle with the Kirsch. Scatter with most of the fresh raspberries, reserving a few for decoration. Pour the white chocolate custard over the Swiss roll and leave to set in the fridge, preferably overnight.

5 To serve, decorate the trifle with the reserved raspberries. Take the piece of white chocolate from the fridge and finely grate over the trifle. Finally, dust with a little icing sugar and place the mint sprigs on top.

Syllabub

SERVES 6–8

Syllabub is one of the great British milk puddings. Once it was made with milk squeezed straight from the cow on to a sweetened wine called 'sill' or 'sille' (from Champagne); this created a froth on top, and it was served as a drink. Sometimes the creamy milk was whipped, which led to the separation of curds and wine after sitting. Today it is made with cream and wine along with some spirit, which makes for a thicker mixture with a slight separation.

Incidentally, they say that a syllabub without brandy is like kissing a man without a moustache...

150ml (5 fl oz) white wine
1 tbsp dry sherry
1 tbsp brandy
finely grated zest of 1 lemon
juice of 2 lemons
freshly grated nutmeg
55g (2 oz) unrefined caster sugar
450ml (15 fl oz) double cream
150ml (5 fl oz) single cream

1 Mix the wine, sherry and brandy in a bowl with the lemon zest, and allow to stand for 2 hours.

2 Strain into a bowl, then add the lemon juice, nutmeg to taste and the sugar. Stir to dissolve the sugar.

3 Whip the double cream into peaks, then carefully stir in the single cream and then the wine mixture. Whisk back to stiffness, but do not over-whip.

4 Pour into chilled glasses and allow to stand overnight until a slight separation occurs in the glasses.

•Some syllabubs used to be made with

cider, and many whisked raw egg white into it to make it lighter.

•Thinking about what I said above. Have you ever tried milking a cow straight into a glass? I should think it's impossible!

Burnt Cream

SERVES 6

There has been constant disagreement as to which came first, the French *crème brûlée* or the English burnt cream. The English version is usually accredited in cookbooks to an original served at Trinity College, Cambridge, dating from about the mid-nineteenth century. But recipes exist from earlier, and in one of 1769, a custard flavoured with orange-flower water is topped with sugar, and caramelised under a salamander. As custards have been part of the British tradition for so long, and sugar became such a passion, I think the British can have a good claim.

1 vanilla pod
600ml (1 pint) double cream
225g (8 oz) unrefined caster sugar

6 egg yolks

1 Preheat the oven to 140°C/275°F/Gas 1 and prepare a bain-marie (a deep roasting tray is fine).

2 Scrape the seeds from the vanilla pod into the cream, add the pod too, then bring up to the boil with 25g (1 oz) of the sugar.

3 Mix the egg yolks in a bowl with 55g (2 oz) of the sugar. Pour the hot cream over, stirring all the time. Put back on to the heat and slowly reheat until the cream starts to thicken.

4 Remove from the heat, and strain into individual ramekin dishes. Put into the bain-marie, pour in enough boiling water to come halfway up the dishes, and bake in the preheated oven for 30 minutes. Take out and cool.

5 Sprinkle the rest of the sugar over the top of each set custard, and put into a trayful of ice. (It may seem a bit of a fiddle, but the ice is really necessary. You don't want the custard to cook any more while the sugar is cooking, and the ice will keep it suitably cool. Brûlées are not meant to be warm...) Put under a well preheated grill until the sugar sizzles, melts and starts to

turn colour.

6 Leave the dishes until the sugar sets, then serve very cold.

Brown Bread Ice-cream

SERVES 6-8

Milk- and cream-based ices are thought to have originated in Italy (an influence of the Arabs in Sicily, perhaps?), then spread through France (where they preferred, and still prefer, water ices) to other parts of Europe. Ice-creams were popular in England from the eighteenth century, and the cream base was often mixed with puréed fruit. Brown breadcrumbs were added then as well, another example of the widespread use of bread in British puddings. The ice-cream may seem to be modern in concept, but history has proved otherwise.

3 egg yolks
115g (4 oz) unrefined soft brown sugar
1 vanilla pod
300ml (10 fl oz) single cream
300ml (10 fl oz) double cream
140g (5 oz) brown breadcrumbs

2 tbsp brandy

1 Whisk the egg yolks and sugar together in a bowl to dissolve all the sugar.

2 Meanwhile, scrape the seeds from the vanilla pod and put them and the pod into a saucepan with the single cream. Bring to the boil.

3 Pour over the egg yolks, stir well, and put back into the pan on a gentle heat, stirring all the time. Allow to thicken slightly then take off the heat. Take out the pod and leave the custard to cool. Cover with clingfilm to prevent a skin forming.

4 Whisk the double cream (not too much) and fold into the cold custard mixture.

5 Preheat the oven to 180°C/350°F/Gas 4.

6 Put the brown breadcrumbs on a tray and toast in the preheated oven for 5 or so minutes. Take out and cool. When the breadcrumbs are cold, mix into the ice-cream mixture with the brandy.

7 Put in a suitable tray, and place in the freezer. When the mixture starts to freeze, stir with a wooden spoon. As the whole tray starts to set, every now and then turn the ice-cream out into a bowl and whisk, then return to the tray and the freezer. Do this until completely set.

8

Bread, Cakes and Baking

The earliest breads would have been rather like oatcakes, ground cereal mixed with water or fat, and baked on heat – at first on hearthstones beside the fire. It wasn't until a form of aeration, or leaven, was discovered that lighter breads became possible. The Romans introduced basic forms of enclosed ovens, and many larger establishments would have had their own, but for many centuries thereafter, the poor still continued to bake bread at the hearth, or take their dough to be baked at a communal bakery.

Plain breads – made from locally available grain – were gradually enriched by flavourings such as spices, and by dried fruits, much as were the pudding mixtures. Bara brith and barm brack are good examples of this, as are teabreads like gingerbread and parkin (both of which can, of course, be found in biscuit form). Small sweet breads were made too, raised by yeast or, later, by chemicals such as baking powder, and baked on the griddle or in an oven. Buns were a further and later development, a cross between an enriched yeast bread and a cake.

At first the dividing line between the two would have been hard to draw. It was only when it was realised that eggs could replace the previous bread yeasts and leavens that cake-making as we know it today properly developed, and cakes are now characterised by their high content of fat and eggs.

Baking seems very *British*, and of course we have two uniquely British institutions – afternoon tea and high tea – at which to enjoy many of its sweet results. High tea is rather more northern, perhaps one reason why the baking tradition has survived so much more successfully in the north of England, Scotland and Wales than it has in the south. There are numerous other theories, many of them quite plausible. And, although the north–south divide is sometimes referred to in disparaging terms, I'm really quite glad that it exists, in that it has ensured the survival of many wonderful breads, cakes and biscuits.

Irish Soda Bread

MAKES 1 ROUND LOAF

Ireland is famous for its simple baking. In the absence of sophisticated raising agents like yeast, and domestic ovens, other means of raising and cooking had to be utilised. At one time buttermilk and other leavens (including sourdough and fermented potato juice) would have raised breads. It was only after the introduction of baking chemicals such as bicarbonate of soda and cream of tartar in the early nineteenth century that the full range of Irish soda breads began to be baked. They are simple to make, but delicious to eat, with butter for breakfast, or as an accompaniment to stews.

Bread such as this would once have been baked on a girdle or griddle or in a frying pan. The bastible, an iron pot with its base in the fire, and hot coals on the lid, was an effective baking oven, still used until very recently in Ireland.

450g (1 lb) flour, half plain white, half
  wholemeal
salt to taste

½tsp each of bicarbonate of soda and
   cream of tartar (or 1 tsp baking powder)
300ml (10 fl oz) buttermilk

1 Lightly grease a baking tray or cast-iron
frying pan, and preheat the oven to
200°C/400°F/Gas 6.

2 Sift the flour, salt to taste, bicarb and
cream of tartar into a bowl. Add the
buttermilk and mix to a dough. Knead and
stretch until smooth.

3 Shape into a round on a floured board,
and roll flat, or use your knuckles, to 4cm
(1½ in) thick.

4 Put on to the tray or into the frying pan,
and cut lightly into quarters (or farls). Bake
in the preheated oven for 25 minutes, then
turn the oven down to 180°C/350°F/Gas 4,
and cook for a further 20 minutes.

5 Take out and wrap in a cloth to keep
soft. Eat quickly, as it does not keep well. In
Ireland, it is made daily and eaten that day.

Bara Brith

MAKES 1 CAKE

The Welsh bara brith, which means 'speckled bread', is very closely aligned to other British fruit loaves – especially the caraway-spiced barm brack of Ireland (the name of which means 'speckled cake'). Both the Welsh and Irish versions were associated with high days and holidays, particularly New Year, inviting comparison with black bun, the Scottish Hogmanay treat, although that is more like a huge 'fly cemetery' cake than a bread.

475g (1 lb 1 oz) plain flour
1 tsp salt
25g (1 oz) unrefined caster sugar
approx. 250ml (9 fl oz) warm milk
25g (1 oz) fresh yeast
1 egg, beaten
½ tsp ground mixed spice
½ tsp ground cinnamon
115g (4 oz) unsalted butter, melted, plus
  extra for greasing
115g (4 oz) currants
55g (2 oz) raisins

1 tbsp treacle
1 tsp caraway seeds

1 Sift 450g (1 lb) of the flour and the salt into a bowl. Make a well in the middle. Mix the sugar and milk together and warm to blood heat, then remove from the heat and crumble in the yeast. Stir to make sure it dissolves. Add to the flour and mix to make a dough. Leave in a warm place to prove until doubled in size, about 40 minutes.

2 Add the egg, spices and melted butter to the dough, then knead and knock back.

3 Cover the dried fruits in the remaining flour, and mix into the dough with the treacle and caraway seeds.

4 Butter a 20cm (8 in) round cake tin and preheat the oven to 180°C/350°F/Gas 4.

5 Split the dough in half, then split one of the halves into two-thirds and one-third pieces. Take the largest half piece, and roll it into a long snake-like shape. Lay this in the cake tin and coil around the inside edge. Do the same with the next largest piece, coiling it inside the first piece. Finally do the same with the smallest piece. Prove in a warm place for about 20 minutes.

6 Bake in the preheated oven for about 1 hour or until golden. Turn out of the tin and cool on a cake rack.

Saffron Bread

MAKES 2 LOAVES

Saffron, the most expensive of spices, consists of the orange-red stigmas of the saffron crocus. These have to be plucked by hand, which is the costly part. Although the spice seems very exotic – it comes mostly now from Spain, India and Iran – the crocuses used to be cultivated in Essex, causing one particular town to affix 'Saffron' to its original name of 'Walden'. Saffron became popular too in the West Country, and saffron cakes – enriched breads really – are still produced there. According to some, the original saffron bread was plain, coloured only by saffron water; the dried fruits were added later.

Eat as an afternoon teabread, sliced with butter. In Cornwall, buns made of this dough were once eaten with clotted cream on Good Friday. However, the best version I have ever had of saffron bread was baked by my friend Clive Davidson at the Champney

Inn at Linlithgow, near Edinburgh. He wrapped the dough round black pudding and rolled it up like Chelsea buns.

a pinch of saffron strands
4 tbsp warm water
300ml (10 fl oz) milk
85g (3 oz) unrefined soft brown sugar
55g (2 oz) unsalted butter
25g (1 oz) fresh yeast
450g (1 lb) plain flour
a pinch of salt
½ tsp freshly grated nutmeg
115g (4 oz) lard, plus extra for greasing
1 egg, beaten
225g (8 oz) currants
115g (4 oz) mixed candied peel
1 tsp finely grated lemon peel

1 Put the saffron to soak in the warm water and leave overnight.

2 Warm the milk in a small pan very gently to blood temperature, then add a pinch of the sugar and the butter. Make sure it's the right temperature – that of a baby's bottle – then crumble in the yeast. Stir to dissolve.

3 Mix the flour, the salt, the rest of the sugar and the nutmeg in a bowl. Rub in the lard until the texture resembles bread-crumbs, then make a well in the centre, pour in the yeast-milk mixture, saffron water and beaten egg, and mix to a dough.

4 Knead until the dough is smooth and elastic in consistency. Put to prove in a warm place, covered lightly (we use clingfilm), until doubled in size, about 1 hour. Meanwhile, use a little of the lard to grease 2 x 450g (1 lb) loaf tins.

5 Knock the dough back, then mix in the dried fruit and peel. Divide between the prepared loaf tins. Prove for a further 30 minutes until risen.

6 Meanwhile, preheat the oven to 200°C/ 400°F/Gas 6.

7 Bake the loaves in the preheated oven for 40–50 minutes. Remove from the heat, and leave to cool in the tin.

•You could use a mixture of equal parts of milk and caster sugar to brush over the top of the loaves as they come out of the oven. This gives a good shine.

•Saffron strands are better to use than powder (which can be adulterated). Don't strain the strands out from the coloured water after soaking, as they give exotic little pools of accentuated colour after baking.

And never use turmeric as a cheaper alternative: the colour may be similar but the flavour is unpleasant.

Hot Cross Buns

MAKES 16

British buns are made from a sweet yeast dough enriched with butter and eggs, dried fruit and spices. The basic mixture for both these hot cross buns, *Chelsea Buns* (see page 276) and many other traditional sweet breads, is similar; the difference lies in what happens thereafter!

When I was a lad I worked during the school holidays, with Frank and Theo, in the Glendale bakery, which sold its product to market stalls. Our busiest time of the year was Maundy Thursday, preparing thousands of hot cross buns for Good Friday. We worked all night, moulding them all by hand (not much technology then...). Frank's late auntie was said to haunt the place, which gave me the willies, but my consolation was as many hot buns as I could eat, straight from the oven.

The cross on hot cross buns, traditionally associated with Easter, can be made simply by cutting into the dough, by piping in a dough mixture, by placing on a cross of separately made pastry, or lines of candied peel.

Basic bun dough
450g (1 lb) plain flour
a pinch of salt
approx. 300ml (10 fl oz) milk
115g (4 oz) unsalted butter
55g (2 oz) unrefined caster sugar
20g (¾ oz) fresh yeast
1 large egg, beaten

Filling
55g (2 oz) currants
55g (2 oz) sultanas
¼ tsp ground allspice
¼ tsp freshly grated nutmeg

Topping
55g (2 oz) plain flour
1–2tbsp water
115g (4 oz) unrefined caster sugar
150ml (5 fl oz) water

1 To make the basic bun dough, sift the flour and salt into a bowl. Make a well in the centre.

2 Very gently warm the milk in a pan, with the butter and sugar, to blood temperature. Take off the heat, make sure it's the right temperature – as for a baby's bottle – then crumble in the yeast. Stir to make sure it dissolves.

3 Add to the well in the flour, along with the beaten egg, and mix to make a dough. Knead well, cover with a cloth, and put in a warm place to prove until doubled in size, usually anything from 20–50 minutes.

4 Knock the dough back and add the dried fruit, allspice and nutmeg. Form into sixteen even-sized balls, and flatten them slightly. Using a sharp knife carefully cut a cross on top of each bun.

5 Mix together the flour and water for the pastry cross. Put into a piping bag, and pipe into the crosses on top of the buns. Place the buns on a greased baking tray, cover and allow to prove until doubled in size, about 30 minutes.

6 Meanwhile, preheat the oven to 220°C/425°F/Gas 7.

7 Bake the buns in the preheated oven for 15–20 minutes. Meanwhile, boil the sugar and water together to make a syrup.

8 Take the buns out of the oven and, while still hot, brush with the syrup to glaze them, giving the buns their characteristic sticky sheen.

•Perhaps the plainest of British buns is the well-known Sally Lunn from Bath. Apart from endless arguments about the origin of the name (is it the name of the baker herself, or derived from *'soleil et lune'*?), the basic dough as here is made up into a sweet bread or buns occasionally enlivened with lemon zest.

•You can add different spices and proportions of dried fruit etc. to the basic bun mixture, and you can also add different toppings. I love those buns with rock sugar on top – Bath buns – and at the Glendale we used to make up 'long buns' with an icing sugar mixture topping, and eat them split with slices of very cold butter.

•It's said in the north of England that if you hang a hot cross bun up in your kitchen it will protect the house from fire for a whole year...

Chelsea Buns

MAKES 16

Made from the same dough as *Hot Cross Buns* (see page 272), Chelsea buns were the speciality of a bakery, The Chelsea Bun House, from the middle of the eighteenth century.

Basic bun dough (see page 273)

Filling and topping
55g (2 oz) unsalted butter, melted
55g (2 oz) unrefined caster sugar
½ tsp ground cinnamon
55g (2 oz) currants
115g (4 oz) sultanas
25g (1 oz) chopped candied peel
2 tbsp icing sugar

1 Make the basic bun dough as described in steps 1–3 of the recipe.

2 Knock the dough back and knead until it is firm, with no air in it. Roll out into a large square about 1cm (½ in) thick.

3 Brush the square with melted butter leaving a 1cm (½ in) margin all around. Sprinkle with the sugar and cinnamon, then the mixed dried fruits and peel, and carefully press these down.

4 Roll up like a Swiss roll and cut into sixteen 2.5cm (1 in) slices. Place these carefully on to a greased, deep-sided baking sheet about 5cm (2 in) apart. Cover with a clean cloth and allow to prove until doubled in size, about 30 minutes.

5 Meanwhile, preheat the oven to 220°C/425°F/Gas 7.

6 Bake the buns in the preheated oven for 15–20 minutes.

7 When taken out, brush immediately with a mixture of icing sugar and enough water to make a single cream consistency. This gives the buns their characteristic white sheen.

•The coiled flat circles of fruity dough are placed together in a tin to bake, when they coalesce, creating the characteristic square shape.

Scotch Pancakes

SERVES 8

Pancakes – thin circles of cooked batter – exist all over Europe (think of the French crêpes), and the batter is very similar to that for Yorkshire pudding. In Scotland, though, what they call 'pancake' is actually a drop scone, made from a thicker batter, raised by baking powder, and cooked on a griddle to a fat circle rather like a crumpet or blini (although the last two are both yeast-raised).

Eat freshly made: they are not so good cold and old. Serve them with cream and jam, or maple syrup or golden syrup and butter.

225g (8 oz) plain flour
1 tsp baking powder
½ tsp salt
25g (1 oz) unrefined caster sugar
1 egg, beaten
1 tbsp golden syrup
approx. 150ml (5 fl oz) milk
25g (1 oz) unsalted butter, melted
vegetable oil for greasing

278

1 Sift the flour, baking powder, salt and sugar together into a bowl, and mix well. Add the beaten egg and golden syrup, along with some milk to make a stiff batter. Add the butter and enough of the rest of the milk to maintain a dropping consistency. Don't be frightened to add a little more milk if you think it needs it.

2 Heat a griddle or frying pan and brush with a little oil.

3 Using a tablespoon, 'drop' an amount on to the griddle and leave to set and colour. Turn over and cook the second side. Each pancake takes about 5 minutes to cook. Store the pancakes inside a tea towel while making the rest.

•A greased metal ring helps to keep the right shape and an even size.

•Although the pancakes are sweet, they go rather well with bacon, but make sure it is a sweet-cure bacon.

•In summer, these pancakes with marinated raspberries and strawberries, topped with clotted cream, make for a real treat.

Scone

MAKES 1 LARGE SCONE

Rather like soda bread (see page 265), a scone mixture would have been raised with buttermilk and cooked on the griddle until the advent of chemical leavens and domestic ovens in the nineteenth century. Varieties of scones are found all over Britain, but the name (pronounced to rhyme with 'gone' in Scotland, 'clone' elsewhere) and the basic concept are claimed as their own by the Scots.

In his café, my dad and his helper, Annie Denton, used to make large scones like this, divided into four farls. They were made to eat then and there, not to be kept.

115g (4 oz) cold butter, diced, plus extra
 for greasing
450g (1 lb) self-raising flour
a pinch of salt
115g (4 oz) unrefined caster sugar
300ml (10 fl oz) milk or buttermilk at
 room temperature, plus extra for brushing

1 Lightly butter a baking tray and preheat

the oven to 200°C/400°F/Gas 6.

2 Sift the flour and salt into a bowl, and quickly rub in the cold butter. Make a well in the centre.

3 Dissolve the sugar in the milk or butter-milk and pour into the well. Gradually stir the flour into the liquid and mix to a dough. Do this as cleanly and quickly as you can. (Speed is of the essence when making scones.)

4 Shape into a large round, brush with milk, and cut a cross in the top.

5 Put on to the baking tray and bake in the preheated oven for 10-15 minutes.

•You can vary scones almost infinitely. The Welsh add 115g (4 oz) extra butter and 225g (8 oz) currants, and I remember Dad used to make date scones. You could also make savoury scones, adding 225g (8 oz) grated Cheddar to the above mixture instead of the sugar.

•In Yorkshire we used to roll our the mixture and cut small shapes out with a fluted cutter to make individual scones. These would take slightly less time to cook.

Parkin

SERVES ABOUT 6–8

Gingerbread has been made in Britain for centuries, and parkin is basically the northern form of gingerbread, but made with the local cereal, oats. Like early gingerbreads, some parkins were made as biscuits, cooked until as hard as most gingerbread men, and on the griddle. Others were made into chemically raised soft sponges that could be baked in the oven, sliced and spread with butter. Different parkins are identified by county names, and this one, inevitably from Yorkshire, and one of the most famous, is traditionally eaten on 5 November. Guy Fawkes was a York man born and bred...

225g (8 oz) fine oatmeal
225g (8 oz) plain flour
1 tbsp ground ginger
½ tsp baking powder
115g (4 oz) unsalted butter
115g (4 oz) unrefined demerara sugar
1 egg, beaten
115g (4 oz) black treacle
115g (4 oz) golden syrup

2 tbsp milk (optional)

1 Line a 20cm (8 in) square baking tray with greaseproof paper and preheat the oven to 160°C/325°F/Gas 3.

2 Mix the oatmeal and flour with the ginger and baking powder, then rub in the butter to a crumb consistency. Add the sugar and beaten egg.

3 Warm the treacle and syrup gently to melt, and add to the mixture. Mix to a paste, using the milk if necessary to achieve a slightly sloppy consistency.

4 Pour the mixture into the prepared baking tray and bake for 1 hour plus. Press the top with the back of a spoon: if it springs back into shape immediately, it is cooked. Take out of the oven and leave to cool a little.

5 After 5 minutes cut into squares, and then leave to cool completely before taking out of the tin.

6 Store in an airtight container for about a week before eating. This is quite important, as the characteristics of the cake change. Eat as a cake.

Gingerbread

MAKES 1 LOAF

Various types of ginger bread, biscuits and cakes exist through Europe – think of the French *pain d'épices* and the German *Lebküchen* and this differentiation is actually found in Britain itself. The famous gingerbread from Grasmere is more like a shortbread, while *Parkin* (see page 282), the northern equivalent of gingerbread, can be biscuit-like or cake-like. Ginger nuts and gingerbread men are the most famous perhaps of the biscuit types (the latter often sold as 'fairings' and eaten on Guy Fawkes Night). Most other gingerbreads are either teabread-like in texture, for slicing and buttering, or richly cake-like as here. It is baked in a loaf tin as a teabread, but it is richer and moister, ideal as a pudding.

Serve cold with fresh fruit and ice-cream, or reheat in a little butter and serve as a pudding with a whisky sauce and perhaps some more diced preserved ginger – or some orange slices caramelised in butter.

115g (4 oz) unsalted butter,

plus extra for greasing

225g (8 oz) plain flour, plus extra for dusting

115g (4 oz) unrefined caster sugar

2 eggs, beaten

225g (8 oz) black treacle, lightly warmed

55g (2 oz) sultanas, finely chopped

85g (3 oz) preserved ginger, finely chopped

2 tsp ground ginger

2 tbsp double cream

½ tsp bicarbonate of soda

1 Butter and flour well a terrine mould or 900g (2 lb) loaf tin, and preheat the oven to 160°C/325°F/Gas 3.

2 Cream the butter and sugar together, then mix in the eggs, treacle, chopped sultanas and preserved ginger.

3 Sift the flour and ground ginger together, and stir into the mixture.

4 Warm the cream slightly, add the bicarb and stir into the mixture.

5 Pour into the prepared mould or tin and bake in the preheated oven for 1½–2 hours.

6 Leave to cool and set in the tin, and then turn out on to a wire cake rack.

Victoria Sponge

MAKES 1 x 2-LAYER CAKE

A true sponge is actually fatless – made from eggs, sugar and flour only – and is so light that it could never be used to hold any type of filling other than jam or some cream. The Victoria sponge, a 'creamed' cake, was created later, obviously named after the old Queen, and included butter 'creamed' with the sugar, and baking powder. (It's the butter that makes it rather crumbly.) I used to make these at school with Elsie Bibby, my teacher. We called them 'jam and cream' sponges, but would sometimes use a butter cream too (icing sugar and unsalted butter). A Victoria sandwich sponge cake is good for tea, along with other cakes and biscuits, but must be very fresh.

  115 g (4 oz) unsalted butter, plus extra for
    greasing
  115g (4 oz) plain flour, plus extra for
    dusting
  115g (4 oz) unrefined caster sugar
  2 eggs, beaten
  ½ tsp baking powder

Filling and topping
about 4 tbsp jam
icing sugar

1 Butter and flour two 18cm (7 in) sponge tins and preheat the oven to 230°C/450°F/Gas 8.

2 Cream the measured butter and sugar together until soft and white. Gradually add the beaten eggs.

3 Sift the flour and baking powder together and lightly fold into the butter mixture.

4 Divide the mixture between the two tins and bake in the preheated oven for 10–15 minutes. Turn out on to a wire cake rack and cool.

5 Spread one sponge with jam and lay the other on top. Dust with icing sugar and serve.

Genoese Sponge

MAKES 1 CAKE

This is actually one of the original types of sponge, being what we call a 'whisked' cake (when the eggs and sugar are first whisked lengthily to incorporate air). It is sturdier than the basic sponge or Victoria sandwich mixture, and less crumbly – it has less butter, but more egg – so I would say this is the cake to use as a vehicle for something else. It's good as a base for fruit and whipped cream, for instance, or in trifle. When I was at the Capital Hotel, we used to soak genoese sponges in sugar syrup flavoured with a liqueur (Kirsch, cherry brandy, Poire William), and then top the almost liquid sponge with fruit and cream. Very popular it was too.

55g (2 oz) unsalted butter, melted, plus extra for greasing
115g (4 oz) plain flour, plus extra for dusting
4 eggs
115g (4 oz) unrefined caster sugar

1 Butter and flour a 23cm (9 in) sponge tin and preheat the oven to 200°C/400°F/Gas 6.

2 Whisk the eggs and sugar together in a bowl over hot water until light, creamy and doubled in size. Take off the heat and whisk until cold.

3 Sift the flour, then carefully fold into the beaten mixture. Fold the melted butter in gently.

4 Pour into the prepared sponge tin and bake in the preheated oven for 25–35 minutes. To test if cooked, run your hand across the top of the cake: the indentations should disappear almost immediately.

5 Leave to cool in the tin, then turn out on to a wire rack.

•There are a few danger signs with sponges:
Too dense a crumb: too much flour, oven too low.
Holes in the mixture: flour not sufficiently folded in.
Sponge sinking or cracked uneven crust: tin filled unevenly, oven too hot.

Dundee Cake

MAKES 1 x 23cm (9 in) CAKE

It is said that this rich and buttery sultana cake came into being through the Dundee marmalade industry. The Keiller family had started their first marmalade factory in 1797, having been inspired by imports of a Portuguese *'marmelo'* or quince paste several generations earlier. They used Seville oranges, which come into season at the end of January. After making the new preserve, the factory might stand unoccupied, so they decided to diversify, and make a cake. They would have established fairly close relationships with Spanish suppliers, so would have access to the almonds and sherry, and two of the cake's defining characteristics, the plump sultanas and candied orange peel, the latter possibly left over from the preserve manufacture. Some Dundee cakes include glacé cherries but, historically, this is a later addition.

225g (8 oz) unsalted butter
225g (8 oz) unrefined caster sugar
4 eggs, beaten

225g (8 oz) plain flour
1 tsp baking powder
85g (3 oz) ground almonds
2 tbsp dry sherry
350g (12 oz) sultanas
115g (4 oz) candied orange peel, chopped
55g (2 oz) blanched whole almonds
1 egg white

1 Grease or line with greaseproof paper a 23cm (9 in) round cake tin, and preheat the oven to 160°C/325°F/Gas 3.

2 Cream the butter and the sugar well together, and slowly beat in the eggs.

3 Sift the flour and baking powder together (keeping back 1 tbsp flour) and add to the mixture along with the ground almonds. Fold in carefully. Add the dry sherry. Mix the sultanas in the remaining 1 tbsp of flour and add to the mix with the orange peel.

4 Spoon into the prepared cake tin, smooth the top and decorate with the blanched almonds.

5 Beat the egg white and brush over the top of the cake. Bake in the preheated oven for 1 hour, then turn the oven down to 140°C/275°F/Gas 1. Bake for another hour plus until cooked through. To test, run a skewer all the way through the cake. If it comes out dry, the cake is ready.

Mince Pies

MAKES ABOUT A DOZEN INDIVI-DUAL PIES OR 1 LARGE PIE TO SERVE 6

Apparently little pies with a filling of *Mincemeat* (see page 312) were associated with Christmas as long ago as the sixteenth century. They were known as 'minced' or 'shred' pies, referring to the actual meat they once contained. I make them now only for Christmas, but my dad served them throughout the year in his café, often making a single large tart.

They say you should eat a mince pie on each one of the twelve days of Christmas, preferably in a different house each time, to ensure twelve happy months in the year to come.

Individual Mince Pies

450g (1 lb) puff pastry
350g (12 oz) *Mincemeat* (see page 312)

milk and unrefined caster sugar to finish

1 Grease a Yorkshire pudding or muffin tray and preheat the oven to 220°C/ 425°F/Gas 7.

2 Roll out two-thirds of the pastry to 3mm (⅛in) thick, Cut into small circles big enough to line the tins, both base and sides, usually about 13cm (5in) in diameter. Fill the pastry-lined tins with mincemeat.

3 Roll out the rest of the pastry to 3mm (⅛ in) thick and cut smaller circles as lids, usually about two-thirds the size of the bases (so about 7.5cm/3 in).

4 Dampen the edges of the bases with water and press the lids on securely. Make two little holes in the middle to allow the steam to escape. Brush with milk and dredge with sugar.

5 Bake in the preheated oven for about 15 minutes. Serve hot with some brandy butter slotted in under the lid.

Large Mincemeat Pie

225g (8 oz) sweet pastry (see *Bakewell Tart* on page 228)
225g (8 oz) *Mincemeat* (see page 312)

milk and unrefined caster sugar to finish

1 Grease a 20–25cm (8–10 in) ovenproof plate and preheat the oven to 220°C/425°F/Gas 7.

2 Take half of the pastry and mould it carefully and quickly into a ball. Roll out to a round of 3mm (in) thick and put on the greased plate. Prick the bottom with a fork, then put in the mincemeat.

3 Roll out the remaining pastry into the same circular shape. Moisten the edges of the pastry round the mincemeat and place the second pastry circle on top. Push down to seal and trim off excess pastry around the plate. Crimp the edges to decorate. Brush with milk and dredge with sugar.

4 Bake in the preheated oven for about 35–40 minutes. Serve hot, again with brandy butter if you like.

•You could use suet pastry to make a mincemeat roly-poly (see the *Spotted Dick* recipe on page 235). Mincemeat would be good in a cheesecake as well.

•Sweet or shortcrust pastry would work as well as puff in the small pies. No reason why not.

Sausage Rolls

MAKES ABOUT 6

Given our British love for sausages and for pastry, it can be no surprise that the two came together. However, despite their continuing appearances on buffet tables, at cocktail and children's parties, and at picnics, I can find no history for them at all. They were a standby in my dad's café, and I remember learning how to make them at grammar school cookery classes, taught by Miss Elsie Bibby every third week.

225g (8 oz) puff pastry
1 garlic clove, peeled and crushed
1 tbsp chopped fresh parsley
450g (1 lb) sausagemeat
salt and freshly ground black pepper
1 egg, beaten with a little water

1 Grease a baking sheet and preheat the oven to 220°C/425°F/Gas 7.

2 Roll out the pastry to a long strip 3mm (⅛ in) thick and 10cm (4 in) wide.

3 Mix the crushed garlic and the parsley with the sausagemeat, and season with salt and pepper. Roll into a sausage shape of about 2.5cm (1 in) in diameter.

4 Lay this sausage on top of the pastry just off centre, closer to the front. Brush the edges of the pastry with water, then fold the pastry over and seal by pushing down carefully.

5 Brush the top with egg wash, then score the top with a fork and brush again with egg wash. Cut the sausage pastry shape into 7.5cm (3 in) lengths.

6 Put on to the greased baking sheet and bake in the preheated oven for about 20 minutes. Serve hot or cold.

•You could make these very much smaller, and serve them as canapés.

•You can vary them in infinite ways. Use shortcrust instead of puff pastry, or indeed filo pastry, which you could deep-fry as you might a spring roll. You can add diced tomato, chilli, cheese, herbs or other spices to the sausagemeat. I've already done that here – my mother would not have countenanced the garlic, for instance… Another idea is to chop up some black pudding with the sausagemeat.

Shortbread

MAKES 2 ROUNDS, ABOUT 16 PIECES

Shortbread biscuits appear all over Britain (in Shrewsbury cakes and the Goosenargh cakes from Lancashire, for instance, both containing caraway seeds), but they are most associated with Scotland. They are 'short' because they contain no liquid, and may be made as 'fingers' or 'petticoat tails'. I've done the latter here, although I haven't cut out a circle from the middle in the traditional way (to prevent broken points to the wedges).

Through John Grant, whose family make Glenfarclas, my favourite whisky, I met James Walker of Aberlour, whose family make the best commercial shortbread. I have encountered him on the odd occasion since, at food exhibitions and the like, and always seem to get a box of shortbread shortly afterwards! Not that I'm complaining...

225g (8 oz) unsalted butter, plus extra for
  greasing
115g (4 oz) unrefined caster sugar, plus
  extra for dredging

225g (8 oz) plain flour
115g (4 oz) rice flour
a pinch of salt

1 Lightly butter a baking sheet and preheat the oven to 160°C/325°F/Gas 3.

2 Cream the measured butter and sugar together until light.

3 Sift the flour, rice flour and salt together, and fold carefully into the butter mixture.

4 Split the mixture in two and shape each half into balls. Flatten each with the hands and put on to the baking sheet. Crimp the edges, then cut across the top, not quite through, into eighths. Prick the centres with a fork.

5 Bake in the preheated oven for 20 minutes, then turn the oven down to 140°C/275°F/Gas 1 and bake for a further 20–30 minutes.

6 Leave to cool. The shortbread will be soft baked at this stage, but as it cools it will crisp up. Dredge with sugar before serving.

•The secrets of shortbread are: use the best ingredients possible (there are so few) and handle the dough as briefly as possible.

Oatcakes

MAKES 2 ROUNDS, ABOUT 16 PIECES

Oatcakes were made all over the country, particularly in the areas where oats flourished – upland Wales, Yorkshire and northwards, and in Scotland. Most were simple amalgams of oatmeal, fat and water as here, some were raised by baking powder, and a few from Derbyshire, Staffordshire and Yorkshire were raised by yeast, making them more like thin drop scones or pikelets than the crisp biscuits we mostly associate the name with.

Oatcakes such as these are delicious with cheese, or for breakfast, but were once the staple diet of many a Scot. In the eighteenth and nineteenth centuries, a Scottish university mid-term holiday was known as 'Meal Monday', allowing the student time to go home and stock up on oatmeal, the source of his porridge, brose and oatcakes while he was away.

115g (4 oz) fine oatmeal
½ tsp salt
1 tbsp melted lard

4 tbsp hot water

1 Mix the oatmeal and salt in a bowl. Add the fat and water and bind together.

2 Roll out to 3mm (⅛in) thick, using extra oatmeal dusted on the work surface. Cut into 7.5cm (3 in) diameter circles.

3 Heat a heavy frying pan or griddle and cook the cakes, with no fat, for 2–3 minutes on one side. Turn over then take off the heat. The residual heat of the pan will finish the second side off.

4 Cool thoroughly, then store in an airtight tin.

9

Preserves, Sauces and Accompaniments

Before refrigeration, a culinary priority was finding a way of preserving ingredients for winter consumption, when fresh produce was unavailable. Meat and fish were salted, dried and smoked from very early on. Many of these techniques were said to have been learned from the invading Vikings although, oddly, we do not seem to have taken to the dried cod and stockfish that they introduced, to such long-lasting effect, in Iberia and the Mediterranean.

The flavours of these preserved meats and fish would have been rather strong, and indeed even fresh meat could probably have been rather high once it was eaten, leading to a generous addition of spices to mask any off tastes. Gluts of vegetables were not mild on the palate either, once preserved in salt and/or vinegar. This enforced familiarity with intensely sharp, salty and spicy flavours may explain why we British have invented and are so keen on all the pickles, ketchups, chutneys and sauces for which we have become renowned. You don't find bottled brown sauce on the Continent, or even the tanginess of mint or horseradish sauces. The famous commercial Worcestershire sauce – believed to be based on a recipe from the East – is another good example of the British penchant for the piquant.

Sweet preserves are a different kettle of fish (so to speak). Gluts of fruit needed to be preserved in much the same way as vegetables, but in a sweet preservative rather than salt or vinegar. Before sugar became more readily available in the eighteenth century, honey would have been used, and sweet quinces, cherries and plums, and sourer gooseberries, crab apples and rose-hips, would have been put in containers to be enjoyed through the winter months. Jams, jellies and marmalade are all examples of this early British culinary thrift, as are what we call fruit 'curds', 'butters' and 'cheeses'.

Early British preserves were made to last, preferably throughout the winter, but today we don't need to bother with that. Try some of these simple recipes – it's good fun! – but eat them up quickly, as there are no E numbers here...

Pickled Onions

MAKES ABOUT 900g (2 lb)

Pickles have been around in Britain for much longer than ketchups or chutneys, and it was probably the taste for spicy, tangy, vinegary pickles that led to the introduction of the other two. Vegetables (and fruit) have been pickled since very early on, as they needed to be preserved for winter eating. The word 'pickle' comes from the German *'pekel'* which means 'brine', apt since most vegetables to be pickled in vinegar are brined first. This reduces the moisture content of the vegetable, ensuring a crisper texture.

Pickled onions are one of the country's favourite pickles, powerfully good with cold meats and with cheese (the proverbial ploughman's). At home we always had some on the table and ate them with fish and chips (you still see pickled onions, eggs and gherkins in chippies), and with meat pies. I think they're quite addictive...

900g (2 lb) small pickling onions (or shallots)

303

115g (4 oz) salt
850ml (1½ pints) water
450ml (15 fl oz) malt vinegar
450ml (15 fl oz) white malt vinegar
1 x 2.5cm (1 in) piece fresh root ginger, squashed
20 black peppercorns
1 tsp ground allspice
2 small fresh red chillies

1 Peel the onions and put them into a bowl.

2 Mix the salt and water together, pour over the onions, and leave to soak for 24 hours.

3 Rinse the onions in fresh water and put them into a sterilised glass jar. Bring the vinegars, ginger, peppercorns, allspice and chillies to the boil together, and pour over the onions.

4 Cool, then cover, and leave in a dark place for four to six weeks before opening and eating.

Tomato Ketchup

MAKES ABOUT 450ml (15 fl oz)

Both tomatoes and the idea of 'ketchup' are fairly new in British culinary terms. The word 'ketchup', which comes from the Chinese name for a fermented fish sauce, did not enter the language until the seventeenth century and tomatoes, although known in Europe in the sixteenth century, did not become familiar (not necessarily *popular*) until well into the late eighteenth century.

Sharp sauces, pickled vegetables and other accompaniments, though, had always been popular, and many gradually acquired the name of 'ketchup', among them mushroom, anchovy, walnut and, eventually, the new-fangled tomato. America was first with its famous, commercially produced tomato 'catsup', and we in Britain have followed enthusiastically, even allying it with our much more traditional fish and chips.

175ml (6 fl oz) red wine vinegar
125g (4 oz) unrefined caster sugar
24 large ripe tomatoes
a couple of dashes each of Tabasco sauce

and Worcestershire sauce

1 Bring the red wine vinegar and sugar to the boil together, stirring until the sugar has dissolved.

2 Meanwhile, skin the tomatoes, remove the seeds, then finely chop the flesh.

3 Add the tomato flesh to the vinegar and boil quickly until the tomatoes 'melt' and the sauce becomes smooth.

4 Remove from the heat and add the two seasoning sauces. Stir in and leave to cool.

•Commercial ketchup is made very differently, but the simplicity of this recipe makes it very special in my book. Because it is so simple, it will not last long.

Fruit Chutney

MAKES ABOUT 1.8kg (4 lb)

Like 'ketchup', 'chutney' is an imported word, derived from the Hindi *'chatni'*, meaning hot or spiced relish, and is a relic of the Raj. In India, the preserve would have been made with mangoes, limes or tamarind, but when the sahibs (or, more importantly, the memsahibs) retired to Britain, they quickly adapted the idea to use native fruit such as apples, pears, plums, gooseberries and green tomatoes.

just over 450g (1 lb) pears
just over 675g (1½ lb) apples
juice of 1 lemon
225g (8 oz) stoned dates
700ml (1¼ pints) malt vinegar
225g (8 oz) onions, peeled
1 fresh red chilli, seeded
1 tbsp salt
1 tbsp ground ginger
½ tsp dry mustard powder
225g (8 oz) unrefined soft brown sugar

1 Wash, peel and core the pears and apples. Make sure you have 1.1kg (2½ lb) in weight.

2 Dice 225g (8 oz) each of the pears and apples, and put to one side in a bowl of water acidulated with the lemon juice.

3 Put the rest of the apples and pears, plus the stoned dates, through the mincer.

4 Put into a pan with the vinegar, bring to the boil and simmer for 10 minutes.

5 Finely chop the onions and chilli and add to the pot along with the salt, ginger, mustard and sugar.

6 Drain and squeeze excess moisture from the diced pears and apples and add to the pan. Simmer for 20 minutes, then allow to cool.

7 Put into sterilised jars, cover with cling-film and non-corrosive lids, and leave for at least 48 hours before eating, and for up to a month or so. As it ages it will become less acid.

•This would go well with curry or cold meats, and I like it in toasted cheese. At Turners we served a chutney like this with a sweetbread terrine.

Banana Chutney

MAKES ABOUT 1.8kg (4 lb)

Bananas could very well have been included in the original Indian chutneys, for they are native to south-east Asia. As they did not travel well from their tropical homelands, they did not become common in Europe until the advent of steamships and refrigerated ships at about the end of the nineteenth and the beginning of the twentieth centuries. I still remember my astonishment at the look and taste of my first banana in the early 1950s, when shipments from the Caribbean started again after the war.

225g (8 oz) sultanas
850ml (1½ pints) malt vinegar
350g (12 oz) unrefined soft brown sugar
1 tsp turmeric
1 tsp curry powder
1 tsp salt
½ tsp ground ginger
225g (8 oz) stoned dates
450g (1 lb) onions, peeled
10 medium bananas, peeled

1 Chop the sultanas and then soak them in the vinegar overnight.

2 The next day, add the sugar, turmeric, curry powder, salt and ginger.

3 Finely chop the dates and onions and add to the other ingredients in a heavy-bottomed pot. Cut the bananas up roughly and add to the pot.

4 Bring up to the boil, then simmer gently until cooked, about 30 minutes. Pot in sterilised jars when cool, and you can eat it virtually straightaway.

•Use as the fruit chutney. It will be slightly sweeter.

Piccalilli

MAKES ABOUT 1.6–1.8kg (3½–4 lb)

Nobody quite knows where this particular pickle got its name, but it must be related to the word 'pickle'. It probably originated later than other traditional British pickles, because it includes so many spices imported from India. The turmeric is used for both flavour and colour, and it is this and the generous use of the British-grown mustard that distinguishes piccalilli from its other relatives.

Our Sunday high tea table when I was a child would always have a jar of home-made piccalilli to go with the cold meats on offer.

450g (1 lb) small cauliflower florets
225g (8 oz) vegetable marrow or courgette, cut into 1cm (½ in) dice
225g (8 oz) small button onions, peeled
450g (1 lb) runner beans, cut into 5mm (¼ in) dice

225g (8 oz) cucumber, cut into 5mm (¼ in) dice
350g (12 oz) salt
1.2 litres (2 pints) white vinegar plus 1 tbsp
a pinch of curry powder
45g (1½ oz) dry English mustard powder
175g (6 oz) unrefined caster sugar
25g (1 oz) piece fresh root ginger, bruised
6 black peppercorns
1 fresh red chilli
25g (1 oz) plain flour
15g (½ oz) turmeric

1 Prepare the vegetables and spread on a deep tray. Sprinkle with the salt and 1.2 litres (2 pints) water, and leave for 24 hours. Rinse and drain.

2 Put the vegetables into a non-reactive pan with the bulk of the vinegar, the curry powder, mustard and sugar. Put the ginger, peppercorns and chilli in a muslin bag and add as well. Bring up to the boil and simmer for 20 minutes.

3 Blend the flour and turmeric with the remaining tbsp of vinegar, add to the mixture, and bring up to the boil. Cook for 3–5 minutes until thickened.

4 Leave to cool, then pot in sterilised jars.

Cover with clingfilm and store in a cool dry place. It can be eaten virtually straight away.

•Piccalilli does mature, though, and you'll often find it has a softer, rounder flavour if you leave it for at least three to four weeks.

Mincemeat

MAKES ABOUT 900g (2 lb)

In the Middle Ages, we British used to love sweet meat mixtures, and mincemeat is actually very medieval in flavour. It would once have contained meat – beef, lamb or offal – but the only remnant of that now is the beef suet. However, as late as the 1860s, Francatelli, chef to Queen Victoria, gave four recipes for mincemeat in his *A Plain Cookery Book for the Working Classes*. These were all price based: the cheapest, at 9d, was made with tripe. Hard to believe, but true. Could you imagine this today?

115g (4 oz) chopped beef suet
115g (4 oz) each of chopped mixed peel, currants, sultanas and raisins
2 apples, peeled, cored and finely diced
175g (6 oz) unrefined demerara sugar

312

finely grated zest and juice of 1 lemon
finely grated zest and juice of 1 orange
1 tsp ground mixed spice
½ tsp freshly grated nutmeg
75ml (2½ fl oz) each of rum and brandy

1 Make sure that all the chopped items are very finely chopped.

2 Mix all the ingredients together, then put into a bowl. Cover with clingfilm, pushing it on to the surfaces of the mincemeat – you don't want any air to get to it.

3 Allow to stand for 1 week in the fridge before using. It could last longer, but it's so delicious I don't think it'll get the chance.

•Use this mincemeat in things like mincemeat roly-poly, mincemeat cheese-cake, and Mince Pies (see page 292).

Strawberry Jam

MAKES ABOUT 1.3kg (3 lb)

Sweet preserves or jams are common and traditional all over Europe. Before sugar became more readily available, in the eighteenth century, honey would have been used to preserve fruits such as quinces, cherries, plums and raspberries. At one time jams would have been made with gluts of fruits, and they would last, hopefully, until the fruit season came round again. That's not so necessary nowadays, but it's still fun to make jam.

Although strawberries are the most difficult of the lot to turn into a jam – they lack the natural pectin vital for a good set – strawberry jam is somehow the one most revered. Lemon juice is used to supply the pectin, as is redcurrant juice, and this recipe, although very simple, is quite delicious.

1.1kg (2½ lb) strawberries
1.3kg (3 lb) unrefined granulated sugar
150ml (5 fl oz) redcurrant juice
juice of 1 lemon
15g (½ oz) unsalted butter

1 Put the strawberries into a large heavy-bottomed pan and heat gently.

2 As the juice starts to come out, add the sugar and stir until dissolved. Add the two juices.

3 Bring the mixture to the boil and remove any scum. Boil rapidly testing for setting point every 15 minutes. Take the pan off the heat to do this.

4 When setting point has been reached, add the butter. Allow the jam to cool slightly before putting into sterilised jars. Before doing this, give the jam a stir to move the fruit around.

5 Keep for a couple of days before eating, and eat within a couple of weeks.

•Individual jams and jellies have individual setting points, which you can test with a sugar thermometer: dip it in hot water, then sink the bulb end into the jam. If the temperature is around 105°C/220°F, the jam has reached setting point.

•However, it is just as simple to keep several small saucers in the fridge. When you think the jam has reached setting point, take the pan off the heat and put a tsp of jam on the cold saucer. Let it cool for a few seconds – count to ten – then push the surface with your finger. If the surface wrinkles, the jam is ready. If the jam is loose, it needs to be boiled for a few minutes more and tested again.

Marmalade

MAKES ABOUT 1.3kg (3 lb)

Marmalade is thought of as very Scottish, but the idea is based on those solid and long-keeping confections popular on the Continent such as the Spanish *'dulce de membrillo'* and the French *'coing'* (in fact quite similar to our own fruit cheeses). The story goes that when Janet Keiller's husband bought some Seville oranges off a ship in their native Dundee at the turn of the eighteenth century, she made a preserve from them. This was based loosely on a recipe for *'marmelo'*, a Portuguese quince paste she had encountered previously. She altered the recipe though, making the preserve less solid, in order to fill more jars – she was a thrifty Scot, after all. (And the Keiller marmalade factory, which was founded thereafter, in 1797, was also where the Dundee Cake – see page 290 – is said to have originated.)

Most of Iberia's Seville orange crop in January is destined for the UK and marmalade manufacture. And, in case you didn't know, Dundee marmalade has shredded peel, while Oxford marmalade uses thick-cut peel...

900g (2 lb) oranges
1.4 litres (2½ pints) water
900g (2 lb) unrefined caster sugar
juice of 2 lemons

1 Wash the oranges well and put in a preserving pan with the water. Slowly boil in the water for around 1½–2 hours then take out and cool. Keep the water.

2 Carefully cut off the peel, leaving the pith behind. Mince or shred the peel – I prefer to mince it.

3 Peel the pith from the oranges with a sharp knife and discard. Take out the pips and wrap them in a muslin bag.

4 Cut the peeled oranges into halves and then slice thinly.

5 Put the orange slices into the orange water, then add the minced peel and the muslin bag of pips. Bring to the boil and simmer for 5 minutes.

6 Take off the heat, then add the sugar and lemon juice. Stir until the sugar has dissolved.

7 Put back on to the heat and bring up to the boil quickly. Test for setting after 15 minutes (see page 315).

8 If the marmalade is ready keep the pan off the heat and allow it to cool for 20 minutes. If not ready, put back on to the heat and bring back to the simmer. Check every 2 minutes.

9 When the marmalade has rested, stir and bottle in sterilised jars.

•Most marmalades are made from Seville oranges, but this one, with less sugar, can be made from ordinary sweet oranges at any time of year.

Apple and Rowan Jelly

MAKES ABOUT 1.3–1.8kg (3–4 lb)

Fruit jellies are wonderful preserves and have long been made by thrifty British housewives. They are a good way of using up gluts of fruit, fruit that is not perfect enough to eat, and a good way of supplying a tart-sweet accompaniment to many other dishes. You can use redcurrants, quinces, crab apples, blackberries, plums or damsons, rosehips, gooseberries, grapes – and indeed herbs (with green cooking apples as the pectin source).

900g (2 lb) apples
1.3kg (3 lb) rowanberries
unrefined granulated sugar

1 Clean the fruit carefully and drain and dry. Cut the apples up roughly.

2 Put into a big pot with enough water just to cover, bring to the boil and simmer gently for 1 hour.

3 Carefully strain the juice through a jelly bag suspended above a bowl. Do not press, as the resultant juice will become cloudy. Be patient.

4 Measure the juice and put into a clean pot. For every 600ml (1 pint) juice, add 450g (1 lb) sugar.

5 Simmer and stir together until the sugar melts, then simmer gently until the jelly reaches setting point (see page 315). Test regularly.

6 Decant into sterilised jars, cool then

cover with clingfilm. The jelly should last well for at least three weeks.

•The principle is the same for most fruit jellies. So long as you have something with pectin in it (apples, lemons etc.), you should be successful. Try any of the fruits mentioned in the introduction above.

Lemon Curd

MAKES ABOUT 450g (1 lb)

The modern lemon curd is of fairly recent origins – the 1800s – and is a direct descendant of the flavoured curd fillings that had been used in pastry tarts since the Middle Ages. Curd, the lumpy protein and fat part of curdled milk (and the basis of most cheeses), was mixed with eggs and flavoured (the lemon only arrived in the late seventeenth century). Yorkshire boasts several curd tarts of this kind, and the famous Richmond Maids of Honour are basically small curd cakes.

Lemon curd was probably developed as a filling for tarts, although gradually it lost the curds, being made only with sugar, butter and eggs, and only very slowly would its other qualities have emerged – its spread-ability on bread or on cake as a filling. You can make fruit curds with a variety of fruit.

My mother used to make lemon curd like this, but she called it 'lemon cheese', a prime example of the confusion there has always been in this area.

225g (8 oz) unrefined cube sugar
4 lemons, washed
115g (4 oz) unsalted butter
2 eggs
2 egg yolks

1 Rub the sugar lumps over three of the lemons to soak up the essential oils from the zest, and put into the top of a double saucepan or a bowl over simmering water.

2 Finely grate the rind of the fourth lemon into the pan, and then add the juice of all the lemons. Add the butter and gently melt these together.

3 Beat the eggs and yolks together lightly. Pour some of the hot mixture into the eggs, stirring continuously, then scrape back into the pan.

4 Heat gently, stirring continuously, until the mixture thickens enough to coat the back of a wooden spoon, about 30 minutes.

5 Leave to cool a little, then pot in small jars. Cover and seal when cold, then store in the fridge for no longer than two to four weeks (if you have the patience – I bet you haven't!).

Sage and Onion Stuffing

SERVES 4–6

A stuffing is hardly a preserve or a sauce, but it is almost as traditional an accompaniment to meats of all sorts as horseradish sauce or piccalilli. Birds and rolled pieces of meat have been stuffed with savoury fillings for centuries. Some of the most classic have got a seasonal nicety about them – the chestnuts with turkey for instance.

2 medium onions, peeled and finely
  chopped
55g (2 oz) pork dripping (lard will do)
1 tbsp chopped fresh sage
115g (4 oz) fresh white breadcrumbs
1 egg, beaten
salt and freshly ground black pepper
25g (1 oz) unsalted butter

1 Preheat the oven to 200°C/400°F/Gas 6.

2 Slowly fry the onion in the lard to soften, but do not colour. Take off the heat and add the sage, breadcrumbs, beaten egg and some salt and pepper.

3 Put in a small buttered ovenproof dish and bake in the preheated oven for 20–30 minutes until well coloured.

•I am cooking the stuffing separately here, but you can of course stuff it into a bird, but remember to do so at the neck end, not in the cavity.

•You could cook the stuffing rolled into individual balls, or you could roll it into a sausage inside foil and roast so that it could be sliced.

•You could add chopped apple or bacon to the basic stuffing, or indeed some chopped dried apricots.

Apple Sauce

SERVES 8

It is said that traditional 'tracklements', or accompaniments, for animals should be made from ingredients on which the animals might have fed. Lamb could possibly have eaten wild mint or redcurrants, I suppose, but I find it hard to think of cattle enjoying horseradish! However, pigs being allowed to wander in apple orchards, eating up the windfalls, is a much more likely scenario, and apple sauce remains a wonderful accompaniment to pork, its sharpness cutting the sweetness and fattiness of the pork. (In Italy, the first food of some suckling pigs is windfall persimmons or sharon fruit, and their flesh is pink, tender and very sweet.)

450g (1 lb) cooking apples
55g (2 oz) unsalted butter
75ml (2½ fl oz) dry cider
a twist of freshly ground black pepper
25g (1 oz) unrefined caster sugar

1 Peel and core the apples. Chop them roughly and put into a non-reactive pan with the cider, sugar and butter. Put on a tight-fitting lid and cook slowly to a purée.

2 Season with black pepper, then pass through a sieve or blend in a liquidiser.

3 Reheat gently to serve.

•If you use dessert apples, leave out the sugar. This is meant to be a tart, not sweet, sauce.

•Try chopping some fresh marjoram into the sauce as you serve.

Mint Sauce

SERVES 4–6

In the Middle Ages, they used to love sweet and sour, herbal flavours in sauces, and this may be a relic of those tastes. Or it could be a reflection of the tradition, found all over Europe, of eating young lamb with bitter herbs (at Easter usually). It's the vinegar content of our mint sauce that the French object to, apparently, forgetting that there are many such sharp sauces in their own cuisine. The sweet redcurrant (or rowan) jelly often eaten with lamb as well (see page 318), can counter-balance the sharpness of the other.

We like mint a lot in this country, often putting a bunch in with the new potatoes or peas. In the north of England we actually eat mint sauce with peas, meat pies and a host of other foods. A famous northern chef was eating in Langan's Brasserie recently, and demanded some mint sauce to eat with his fish, chips and mushy peas. Nobody blinked...

3 tbsp chopped fresh mint leaves
1 tbsp unrefined caster sugar
freshly ground black pepper
150ml (5 fl oz) white malt vinegar (or
   white wine vinegar)

1 Mix the mint with the sugar in a bowl, and give it a couple of good turns of the peppermill.

2 Stir in the vinegar and do a taste test. If it is too sharp, add a dash of water. Use within a couple of hours.

Horseradish Sauce

SERVES 6

Horseradish was introduced to Europe from Asia, and to Britain from Germany apparently, where they use it a lot in sauces. Although we think its association with roast beef must be as old as the hills, it seems only to have been around since the beginning of the nineteenth century.

The flavour is incredibly pungent, but is the pain of peeling and grating worth it? The grated stuff in jars is fine, and is easy to find and use along with the other ingredients.

25g (1 oz) freshly grated horseradish
1 tbsp white wine vinegar
150ml (5 fl oz) double cream
salt and freshly ground black pepper
a squeeze of lemon juice

1 Mix the horseradish and vinegar together.

2 Lightly whip the cream, then season it with salt, pepper and lemon juice.

3 Mix the horseradish and cream mixtures together well. Use within a day or so.

•Stand well back when you peel and grate fresh horseradish root, as the effect is ten times worse than peeling the strongest onion!

•Use horseradish or horseradish sauce in various ways. It's particularly good with smoked meats or perhaps surprisingly, smoked fish. It can also be added to mashed potatoes, and a horseradish mash can be made into a potato cake and fried like bubble and squeak.

Cumberland Sauce

SERVES 8

It was Elizabeth David who suggested that this sauce might have been named after Queen Victoria's uncle, the Duke of Cumberland. As the sauce is very German in feel, and he was the last independent ruler of Hanover, this could be correct. The recipe also first appeared in cookery books during Victoria's reign, and became a vital accompaniment to game dishes. We serve it with ham mostly now, but it's good with any cold meat. At The Capital we served scallop mousse with horseradish and Cumberland sauce.

Oxford sauce is very similar, but uses only the zest of the orange, not the juice.

1 orange
1 shallot, peeled and finely chopped
juice of ½ lemon
150ml (5 fl oz) port
a pinch of cayenne pepper
350g (12 oz) redcurrant jelly

1 Cut the zest from the orange, leaving behind any pith, and then cut it into fine julienne strips. Squeeze the juice from the denuded orange.

2 Put all the ingredients except the jelly into a pan and slowly simmer to reduce to one-third of its original volume. Pour into a bowl.

3 Whisk or liquidise the redcurrant jelly, then pour into the bowl. Mix well.

Wine Sauce

SERVES 4

There's nothing particularly British about this wine sauce, although we have been flavouring sauces with wines for centuries. In the Middle Ages it was verjuice, the juice of unripe grapes (all English grapes were good for, I should think).

This simple and straightforward sauce was taught to me by Eric Scamman, my mentor at The Savoy, and can add flavour and texture to many dishes. Make it with white wine, red wine, sherry, port or Madeira, or even with Cognac.

25g (1 oz) unsalted butter
2 shallots, peeled and finely chopped
300ml (10 fl oz) wine or spirit of choice
150ml (5 fl oz) white wine
600ml (1 pint) veal stock
115g (4 oz) butter, cold and chopped
salt and freshly ground black pepper
1 tsp fécule (potato flour), slaked in 1 tbsp
   white wine

1 Melt the unsalted butter in a pan, add

the shallots, and sweat to soften, but do not colour.

2 Add your chosen wine or spirit, plus the white wine. Bring to the boil and reduce to nearly nothing, to what we call a syrup.

3 Add the veal stock to this intensely flavoured syrup, bring to the boil and reduce by one-third.

4 Shake in the chopped cold butter and check the seasoning.

5 Thicken slightly over a gentle heat, using the fécule and white wine.

6 Pass through a fine sieve and serve.

•As to which sauce to serve with which meats, there are no real rules. A red wine sauce goes with the big red meats, beef and lamb. A white wine sauce is good with pork or chicken. A Madeira sauce is ideal with fillet of beef, or *Beef Wellington* (see page 129), and a port sauce accompanies kidney, liver and game birds. Cognac is good with kidneys, chicken and beef, and sherry is delicious with offal, chicken and pork.

Custard Sauce

SERVES 4–6

Eggs and milk are basic ingredients in any cuisine, and most countries have several custard dishes. The English name comes from 'crustade', meaning a pastry case, in which custards were originally cooked (and Fullerton's in Morley High Street still sells custard tarts to die for). The sauce evolved from the baked puddings, and has become so indissolubly associated with Britain that the French call it *'crème anglaise'*. An accolade indeed!

This is a rich version, and although it is a little more difficult to make than simply opening a tin or carton, or mixing custard powder with milk (how times have changed!), it's well worth it.

450ml (15 fl oz) milk
300ml (10 fl oz) double cream
1 vanilla pod
6 egg yolks
4 tbsp unrefined caster sugar

1 Put the milk and double cream into a

pan. Scrape the vanilla seeds from the pod into the pan, add the pod as well, and bring up to the boil. Pull to one side of the stove, off the heat.

2 Meanwhile, whisk the egg yolks, then add the sugar, and whisk until the sugar has dissolved.

3 Pour the warm milk over the egg yolks and stir well. Put back into the pan and, stirring continuously with a wooden spoon, bring back to heat, but do not boil. (A double boiler might be safer, if you have one.)

4 When the custard thickens sufficiently to coat the back of the wooden spoon, about 4–5 minutes, take off the heat and pour into an old-fashioned custard jug.

•If not using the sauce immediately, put a piece of buttered greaseproof on the top of it to prevent a skin forming. Or use a butter wrapper – waste not, want not!

•To re-use, either hot or cold, mix with some double cream. Even more luxurious!

Acknowledgements

Thanks are due to a number of people, not least all those who have written about British food over the last few decades, and whose expertise was invaluable in my researches. I am hugely grateful to my editor, Susan Fleming, who pulled it all together and made it fun. Thanks also to my agent Laura Morris, to the Headline gang – particularly Heather Holden-Brown, Lorraine Jerram and Bryone Picton -- and to those involved in the wonderful photography: William Shaw, Lisa Pettibone, Annabel Ford and Roisin Nield. A special mention too for the team at designsection, who have made the book look great. Finally a big thank you to Jon Jon Lucas, Gerard O'Sullivan and Paul Bates for their help in advising and testing recipes, to Louise Hewitt in the office and, last but not least, to my wife and sons.

The publishers hope that this book has given you enjoyable reading. Large Print Books are especially designed to be as easy to see and hold as possible. If you wish a complete list of our books please ask at your local library or write directly to:

Magna Large Print Books
Magna House, Long Preston,
Skipton, North Yorkshire.
BD23 4ND